The Bible in Counseling:

A Guide to Effective Counseling Ministry Through the Use of Scripture

*By
Stan E. DeKoven*

Copyright © 2009 by Dr. Stan E. DeKoven

ISBN: 978-1-61529-007-9

All rights in this book are reserved worldwide. No part of this book may be reproduced in any manner whatsoever without the written permission of the author except brief quotations embodied in critical articles or reviews.

Published by:

Vision Publishing

1115 D Street

Ramona, CA 92065

www.visionpublishingservices.com

1-800-9-VISION

All scripture references are taken from the
NASB version of the Bible unless otherwise noted.
Printed in the United States of America

Acknowledgements

There have been many organizations that have developed valuable guides to biblical counseling; of special note is the "CBN Counselor Handbook, 20th Anniversary Version" and "Meat for Christians" by Gylord Evangelistic Ministries, Inc.

Rather than fully recreate the wheel, I have gleaned much from their model, adding to them my specific emphasis; and having modified the categories as needed.

I am always grateful for those who have done pioneer work, and am hopeful that this volume will be a blessing to students and counselors alike.

Finally, my special thanks to two colleagues. First, to Delores Horsman, M.A., a gifted counselor and minister for Christ, who helped immeasurably with the editing of this work, and secondly to Dr. Richard Walters, Dean of the College of Counseling for Vision International University, who gave excellent suggestions in terms of categories needed and not. To both of you, thanks.

Stan DeKoven, Ph.D.

Using This Manual

As this book is written for counselors to use, it presents common problems from a counselor's viewpoint. Included are definitions of the problems to be faced, a general commentary on how to deal with the problem from a Christian Counselors view, and scriptures that can be used to assist the client you might be working with to integrate your words of wisdom and counsel with biblical revelation. Further, where an * is found at the end of a problem description, a reference book is provided in the back of this volume to assist you in further study and often to be used as a resource for your clients to help them grow. I trust this will be a tool that will bless you in your work. It is a growing resource, and will be frequently edited to add and update for the benefit of the counselors, thus your input is solicited for future editions. More on this at the end of the book.

Table of Contents

Introduction 9
ABUSE 19
ADULTERY 20
ALCOHOL 21
ANGER 23
ANXIETY 24
ASSURANCE 26
ATTITUDE 27
BAD HABITS 29
BEAUTY 31
BITTERNESS 32
BORN AGAIN 34
CALLING 35
CHURCH 37
COMPASSION 39
CONCEIT 40
CONFESSION 41
CONFIDENCE 43
CONFORMITY 44
COURAGE 46
DEATH 47
DEFEAT 49
DECISIONS 50
DEMONS 52
DEPRESSION 53
DISCOURAGEMENT 55
DIVORCE 56

DOUBT	58
DRUG ABUSE	59
ENEMIES	60
ETERNITY (See Heaven below)	
ENVY/JEALOUSY	61
FAITH	63
FEAR	65
FORGIVENESS	66
FRIENDS	69
FUTURE	71
GIFTS FROM GOD	72
GIVING	74
GLUTTONY	75
GOALS	77
GRIEF	78
GUILT	79
HEALING	81
HEAVEN	83
HOME	84
HOMOSEXUALITY	86
HONESTY	88
HOPE	90
HUMILITY	91
INCEST	93
LONELINESS	95
LOVE	97
LUST	99
MARRIAGE	101

MIRACLES	104
MONEY	105
OBEDIENCE	107
PARENTS	109
PATIENCE	110
PEACE	111
PERSECUTION	112
PRAYER	114
PRIDE	115
RESURRECTION	117
REVENGE	119
SALVATION	120
SATAN	122
SELF IMAGE	123
SEXUAL IMMORALITY	126
SHAME	128
THANKFULNESS	129
THOUGHTS	132
TROUBLE	133
TRUST	134
WISDOM	135
WORRY (See Anxiety, page 4)	
WORSHIP	137
Conclusion and Recommendations	139

Introduction

In order to establish a biblical foundation for counseling, it is necessary to review the Hebrew understanding of psychology.

Psychology as the "science" or knowledge of the mind did not exist for the O.T. Hebrew. The Jew of the O.T. was not concerned with knowledge in the way that we today understand it. To obtain knowledge was to gain understanding.

"If you seek her as silver, And search for her as for hidden treasures; Then you will discern the fear of the Lord, And discover the knowledge of God. For the Lord gives wisdom; From his mouth come knowledge and understanding." (Proverbs 2:3-6)

The whole goal of gathering knowledge was so that one might gain understanding and a more complete knowledge of God. The O.T. Hebrew understood that all knowledge, all wisdom, all understanding was discovered in the knowledge of God and His Word.

The Hebrew knew that,

"How blessed is the man who finds wisdom; And the man who gains understanding. For its profit is better than the profit of silver, and its gain than fine gold. She is more precious than jewels; And nothing you desire compares with her. Long life is in her right hand; In her left hand are riches and honor. Her ways are pleasant ways, and all her paths are peace. She is a tree of life to those who take hold of her. And happy are all who hold her fast." (Proverbs 3:13-18)

All that any person could ever want in life is listed in these five short verses; Happiness, riches, honor, pleasantness, peace, and eternal life. When King Solomon could ask from God anything he wanted, he chose wisdom. (I Kings 3:5-12) In Psalm 119:99-100 David says,

"I have more insight than all my teachers, for Thy testimonies are my meditation. I understand more than the aged, because I have observed Thy precepts."

God's revelation to us was not made for a primarily intellectual purpose. "To know" in the Hebrew sense means to mirror the reality of something in one's consciousness. The biblical idea is to have the reality of something practically interwoven with the inner experience of life. Hence "to know" can stand for the word "to love" "to single out." The Word is the highest and noblest function of man, the highest expression of worship, and is therefore identical with his action.

For the Hebrew, the goal of knowledge was to gain understanding of God. The goal of understanding was that one might obtain wisdom to know how to walk in a manner pleasing to the Lord. Life for the Hebrew was "covenant" a relationship with God and with his brothers. The goal of that life is the working out of that covenant. It is as he lived rightly related to God and others that he would experience the promised blessings. It is interesting to note that the wisdom after which the Hebrews sought was the "wisdom which comes from above," (James 1:17). It was a wisdom that came through the revelation of the Word. It was not a wisdom that came through the mind or through nature. The origin of this wisdom could be known by its fruits. (James 3:13-18).

It is key to understand that wisdom, which will produce happiness, riches, honor, etc..., comes only through the revelation of the Word.

We as Christians do not need to look to the knowledge of men, but to the wisdom which cometh from above. The scripture says plainly,

"But if any of you lacks wisdom, let him ask of God, who gives to all men generously, and without reproach; and it will be given to him." (James 1:5)

The Word of God – the Interrogator

"For the Word of God speaks, is alive and full of power making it active, operative, energizing and effective; it is sharper than any two-edged sword, penetrating into the dividing line of the life (soul) and (the immortal) spirit; and of joints and marrow, (that is the deepest part of our nature) exposing the sifting and analyzing and judging the very thoughts and purposes of the heart." (Hebrews 4:2, amp.)

It is the Word of God that acts as a surgical instrument in the counseling situation. It reveals to us what is in the deepest resources of our hearts. It is a delicate and powerful instrument in the hand of the counselor and should be used skillfully.

Use of the Scripture in Counseling

Again, The Psalmist wrote, "I have more insight than all my teachers for your testimonies are my meditation," (Psalm 119:99).

Use of scriptures in counseling involves gaining a biblical understanding of the person's problem while examining all relevant data in the light of God's Word. There is no shortcut to letting "the Word of Christ richly dwell within you," (Colossians 3:16).

The goal is to bring together the person's problem and God's solution, for in fact, there are no problems without solutions, (I Corinthians 10:13).

Thus, it may require making a biblical plan of action, e.g., with women who have unsaved husbands, (I Peter 3:1).

Further, the bible is able to teach the counselee how to use the scriptures in problem solving, through implementing a concrete plan of action, e.g., the person who has a bad temper and says that they cannot change. The Scripture says that one aspect of the fruit of the Spirit is self-control. Ephesians 4:25-32 lays out a plan of action for practical change including: (a) daily communication, while not allowing the sun to go down on your out of control or unreasonable anger; (b) use only words that build-up and not tear down; and (c) forgive, rather than slander, gossip, or attack with words that hurt and offend."

The Human Channel - Counselor

"For God who said, "Light shall shine out of darkness", is the One who has shone in our hearts to give light of the knowledge of the glory of God in the face of Christ. But we have this treasure in earthen vessels, that the surpassing greatness of the power may be of God and not from ourselves," (II Corinthians 4:6-7).

There is power available to us, the same power which brought about the creation of all life. We are only the vessels, the channel through which that power flows. Here we have both hope and humility, a balance which always needs to be maintained.

We have the Holy Spirit and the Word of God to do the job to which He has called us. "Faithful is He who calls you, and He also will bring it to pass.," (I Thessalonians 5:24).

Questions should help the counselee to think and explore rather than just to answer "yes" or "no." Questions beginning with "who," "what," "where," and "when" are often helpful. Another source of necessary information to help can include an inventory, which the person can fill out prior to the counseling session. This can include certain basic information as well as questions of "What would you like to accomplish through our time together," or "What is the main problem as you see it?" With every counselee there is certain vital information which will be gathered over a period of time, this includes:

Who is She/He? – Identity

It is so beautiful, as we read through the Gospels, to observe how Jesus ministered to people. The scripture tells us that he knew their hearts, and it is obvious that he treated each one just a little differently. He knew who they were and was flexible in his method of dealing with them. Every person is unique and must be respected and treated in keeping with that uniqueness. We need to ask the Holy Spirit to give us eyes to see this person as He sees them and not as they may appear to be.

Where Has He/She come from? – History and Development

Most people come into the Kingdom of God with significant deficits and wounds caused by the world system. The scripture says, "...forgetting what lies behind and reaching forward to what lies ahead, I press on toward the goal for the prize of the upward call of God in Christ Jesus." (Philippians 3:13-14). This was Paul the apostle's aspiration, to forget the past in such a way that it had absolutely no hold on him. This putting away of the past however, is not a mechanical operation. Before the past can be forgotten, it must **first be reconciled**. That is, hurts, fears, even triumphs must be seen in light of scripture, neither enemy nor friend. We must make peace with the person of our past. We must remember that it is that person that Jesus saw fit to die for.

Because God has forgiven us, we must forgive ourselves. To forgive means that the debt has been paid and the debtor's prison door has been opened. It is important in counseling to understand where the person is in regard to their past and especially in regard to personal reconciliation. II Corinthians 5:17-19 says,

"Therefore, if any man is in Christ, he is a new creature: old things passed away; behold, new things have come. Now all these things are from God, who has reconciled us to himself through Christ, and has given to us the ministry of reconciliation; namely, that God was in Christ, reconciling the world to himself, not counting their trespasses against them; and has committed to us the word of reconciliation."

God has provided a way for old things to truly pass away and for all things to become new. This way is through the **ministry of reconciliation**, another aspect of the ministry of counseling. The counselor must ask the question: "How can I best help this person to experience reconciliation with their past, in their relationships, with God and man?" The answer to this question comes through knowledge of the person, their history, and the Word of God as directed by the Holy Spirit.

Where is she/he going? – Goals

"Do you not know that those who run in a race all run, but only one receives the prize? Run in such a way that you may win. I run in such a way as not without aim; I box in such a way, as not beating the air:" (I Corinthians 9:24,26). Also Proverbs 29:18 says, "Where there is no vision, the people are unrestrained, but happy is he who keeps the laws." Many people who come for counsel are void of direction, without goals. Sadly, many have lost their hope. Often, they do not understand the principles of God's word or how to walk in the wisdom that the Word of God provides. Thus, another aspect of the counselor's ministry is to help the counselee have their hope restored, and learn what God's word says and how to apply it. Proverbs 10:28 says, "The hope of the righteous shall be gladness."

It is never appropriate to bludgeon a person with condemning words, even scriptural ones. If they are seeking help, especially voluntarily, they are already wounded, open and vulnerable. Gentleness, allowing room for conviction (from the Holy Spirit) not condemnation (from the flesh or the 'devil'), will be a blessing to the counselee. Of course, it is not enough to have intellectual knowledge of scripture, but it must be practically applied (the counselor may/should come up with suggestions to apply the word in practical ways). This takes wisdom, common sense and practice, whether you are doing phone counseling or face-to-face.

Problems are not People; People are not Problems

As we turn towards the meat of this book, it is important to remember that people have problems, and problems can have (as in to dominate) people. Essentially, people are more than their problems just as the principle of scripture (or Spirit) is infinitely more important than the letter (the letter kills, but the Spirit gives life, II Corinthians 3:6).

Thus, in using the scriptures referenced in this book, remember that the person you are talking with is your central focus. He/She deserves your very best, is created in the image of God and is intimately loved by Him. He/she requires your attention, listening ear and kind intention as you share with them biblical solutions. Again, try to listen for the root problem, not just the surface presentation. For instance, if they are contemplating having an abortion, telling them what God says about the topic and encouraging acceptable alternatives is most appropriate (as well as a referral for counseling). However, if they have had an abortion, it is important to ascertain their feelings, perceptions about their behavior (anger, guilt, fear of judgment, self justification), and then present a more biblical solution (forgiveness, repentance, accepting responsibility without condemnation, grief and mourning).

Once you have presented the scripture and talked through its meaning, always encourage acting on their new information: This can include

- Prayer
- Referral
- Restitution
- Church, etc...

Action is necessary, not just insight.

A word of caution is needed: know when to refer. If someone is suicidal, is a child thought to be abused, or a woman in a volatile domestic situation, don't try to be hero. Often the best counsel we can give is a well informed and professional referral.

A Final Word

Who Is The Counselor?

The scriptures indicate (John 14-16; II Cor. 1) that the Paraclete, the Holy Spirit, is our divine counselor leading us into all truth. Further, Paul stated that all believers as paracletes (counselors/comforters) are to assist others in the areas where comfort, courage, strength or counsel has been received from God.

Thus, the approach for Christians as equipped counselors is to rely on the Word of God for guidance, combined with practical wisdom, as guided by the Holy Spirit to assist fellow strugglers on their road to change, growth and maturity.

As such, trust the Lord. He is willing and able to assist you in your ministry. Remain teachable, always learning, so that you can fulfill your destiny in God while blessing others through your words, and loving deeds.

Now we move on to some specific, though not comprehensive, problems often faced by the counselor in the counseling office.

ABUSE

Definition:

To use wrongly or improperly; misuse: *abuse alcohol; abuse a privilege*. Also, to hurt or injure by maltreatment; ill-use. Another definition would be to force sexual activity on; rape or molest; to assail with contemptuous, coarse, or insulting words; revile.

Brief Explanation:

Sadly, abuse is often found in families in the church, and the church is a microcosm of the world, though forgiven. Many patterns of family life, previous abuse or neglect, occurring before salvation are brought with the believer into the church, and can be acted on. When physical, sexual or emotional abuse occurs, whether towards child or spouse, safety must be considered first. God's word speaks to the harm of abuse, and God's ability to forgive and heal. For more, see *Family Violence: Patterns of Destruction by Dr. DeKoven.*

The Word of God:

Psalm 34:4,5

"I sought the Lord, and He answered me, And delivered me from all my fears. They looked to Him and were radiant, And their faces shall never be ashamed."

1 Peter 5:7

"...casting all your anxiety upon Him, because He cares for you."

Psalm 42:11

"Why are you in despair, O my soul? And why have you become disturbed within me? Hope in God, for I shall yet praise

Him, the help of my countenance, and my God."

Genesis 6:11

"How the earth was corrupt in the sight of God, and the earth was filled with violence."

Luke 3:14

"And some soldiers were questioning him, saying, "And what about us, what shall we do?" And he said to them "Do not take money from anyone by force, or accuse anyone falsely, and be content with your wages."

ADULTERY

Definition:

Voluntary sexual intercourse between a married person and a partner other than the lawful spouse.

Brief Explanation:

In our day of lower standards of morality, adultery and other forms of sexual immorality are pandemic. With easy access to the internet and other forms of temptation, remaining pure is more difficult than perhaps at any other time. Further, due much to the changes in expectations in relationship (I deserve great sex all the time, whenever I want), when "needs" are not met, options for other relationships not approved by God are explored. When adultery or other forms of unrepented immorality occurs, trust is violated, and the offender must be confronted with truth, sin must be repented of, and healing, if possible, must be pursued. See *Marriage and Family Life: A Christian Perspective* by Dr. Stan DeKoven.

The Word of God:

Proverbs 6:32

"The one who commits adultery with a woman is lacking sense; He who would destroy himself does it.

Matthew 5:27,28

"You have heard that it was said, 'You shall not commit adultery'; but I say to you, that everyone who looks on a woman to lust for her has committed adultery with her already in his heart."

Luke 16:18

"Everyone who divorces his wife and marries another commits adultery; and he who marries one who is divorced from a husband commits adultery."

Matthew 15:19

"For out of the heart come evil thoughts, murders, adulteries, fornications, thefts, false witness, slanders."

Proverbs 28:13

"He who conceals his transgressions will not prosper. But he who confesses and forsakes them will find compassion."

1 John 1:9

"If we confess our sins, He is faithful and righteous to forgive us our sins and to cleanse us from all unrighteousness."

ALCOHOL

Definition:

Alcohol is a colorless volatile flammable liquid, C_2H_5OH, synthesized or obtained by fermentation of sugars and starches and widely used, either pure or denatured, as a solvent and in drugs, cleaning solutions, explosives, and intoxicating beverages. For our purposes, it is intoxicating liquor containing alcohol. It is not specifically the usage of alcohol, but the abuse of it that is a great problem in Western culture.

Brief Explanation:

Alcohol use is not forbidden in scripture, but the abuse of it clearly is. When alcohol becomes a problem, help is readily available. Of course, though help is readily available, often it is not availed of due to the defense mechanism known as denial. The alcoholic denies the need for help.

Alcohol abuse does not only affect the health of the person abusing the substance, but also the family and friends. It is an insidious problem, yet God can heal. All members of the family will need help, support and strength, but families who deal with the denial, confront the abuser and if the abuser receives help, healthy family life is more than possible. For more, see *Addictions Counseling and 12 Steps to Wholeness* by Dr. Stan DeKoven

The Word of God:

Proverbs 20:1

"Wine is a mocker, strong drink a brawler, and whoever is intoxicated by it is not wise."

Proverbs 23:20, 21

"Do not be with heavy drinkers of wine, Or with gluttonous eaters of meat;"

1 Corinthians 6:9,10

"Or do you not know that the unrighteous shall not inherit

the kingdom of God? Do not be deceived; neither fornicators, nor idolaters, nor adulterers, nor effeminate, nor homosexuals, nor thieves, nor the covetous, nor drunkards, nor revilers, nor swindlers, shall inherit the kingdom of God."

Ephesians 5:18

"And do not get drunk with wine, for that is dissipation, but be filled with the Spirit..."

ANGER

Definition:

A strong feeling of displeasure or hostility. A biological response to frustration, hurt or fear.

Brief Explanation:

Everyone becomes angry at times, but it is expressed in either healthy or unhealthy ways. Bill was a preacher who had a problem with rage. Due to his great insecurity, whenever he performed at a less than perfect way, he would rage at himself, or if someone disagreed with him on something, mostly minor issues, he would scream and threaten. Of course, he did not just need anger management, that is, help in learning healthy ways of expressing anger, but he needed to repent and seek help for his lack of emotional security, coming into a fuller understanding of his identity being in Christ and not in his own competence. Angry words can be most damaging to children and spouses, church members and friends.

The Word of God:

Proverbs 29:11

"A fool always loses his temper, But a wise man holds it back."

Matthew 5:21, 22

"You have heard that the ancients were told, 'You shall not commit murder' and 'Whoever commits murder shall be liable to the court.' But I say to you that everyone who is angry with his brother shall be guilty before the court; and whoever shall say to his brother, 'Raca,'' shall be guilty before the supreme court; and whoever shall say, "You fool,' shall be guilty enough to go into the fiery hell."

Ephesians 4:26, 27

"Be Angry, and yet do not sin; do not let the sun go down on your anger, and do not give the devil an opportunity."

ANXIETY

Definition:

A state of uneasiness and apprehension, as about future uncertainties. A cause of anxiety, such as air travel for some people, is a truly debilitating state. In psychological terms, anxiety is a state of apprehension, uncertainty, and fear resulting from the anticipation of a realistic or fantasized threatening event or situation, often impairing physical and psychological functioning.

Brief Explanation:

Anxiety is psychological pain, and it is very real and potentially devastating. There are many different expressions of anxiety, from a sense of dread to debilitating phobias or panic responses. The root of anxiety is generally a wrong interpretation of thoughts that bombard the mind of the person. Taking authority over ones thoughts is the goal, conforming the thoughts to God's work the key; but again, as with many areas of difficulty, this is easier said than done.

For those with minor anxiety, simply talking about the problems one is facing can help, as can prayer for God's intervention. Often confronting the negative beliefs that are inevitably a part of the anxiety can help.

Where the problem is more insidious, cognitive psychology can be an effective tool in helping someone with overwhelming anxiety, and professional help may be required. God is certainly able to help someone with anxiety, and his word, meditated upon consistently can make a major and dramatic difference for many.

The Word of God:

Proverbs 3:5,6

"Trust in the Lord with all your heart, And do not lean on your own understanding. In all your ways acknowledge Him, And He will make your paths straight."

Psalm 42:11

"Why are you in despair, O my soul? And why have you become disturbed within me? Hope in God, for I shall yet praise Him, The help of my countenance, and my God."

Psalm 34:4

"I sought the Lord, and He answered me, And delivered me from all my fears."

Ephesians 5:18

"Cast your burden upon the Lord, and He will sustain you; He will never allow the righteous to be shaken."

Philippians 4:6,7

"Be anxious for nothing, but in everything by prayer and supplication with thanksgiving let your requests be made known to God. And the peace of God, which surpasses all comprehension, shall guard your hearts and your minds in Christ Jesus."

Romans 8:28

"And we know that God causes all things to work together for good to those who love God, to those who are called according to His purpose."

ASSURANCE

Definition:

> The act of assuring; of presented as a statement or indication that inspires confidence; a guarantee or pledge: *gave her assurance that the plan would succeed.* Also, freedom from doubt; certainty: *set sail in the assurance of favorable winds.* Some synonyms can help in our understanding, such as self-confidence or as a believer, confidence in God and His word.

Brief Explanation:

Dr. Richard Walters in his book *Off Center, Off Course* (available from www.highgroundpress.org) provides an excellent explanation of those who never find the peace Jesus promised in the knowledge of their salvation. This can come due to a wrong belief about salvation (by grace we are saved, not of works) and God's ability to sustain us until we go to be with the Lord. If one has asked Christ into their lives with sincerity, they can be assured of his presence with them and his ability to sustain them until they go to heaven. Prayer to assist the honest doubter is most helpful, as is an understanding of the scriptures presented here.

The Word of God:

John 3:36

"He who believes in the Son has eternal life; but he who does not obey the Son shall not see life, but the wrath of God abides on him."

Job 19:25-27

"And as for me, I know that my Redeemer lives, And at the last He will take His stand on the earth. Even after my skin is destroyed, Yet from my flesh I shall see God; Whom I myself shall behold, And whom my eyes shall see and not another. My heart faints within me."

Romans 8:38, 39

"For I am convinced that neither death, nor life, nor angels, nor principalities, nor things present, nor things to come, nor powers, nor height, nor depth, nor any other created thing, shall be able to separate us from the love of God, which is in Christ Jesus our Lord."

Philippians 4:6,7

"Be anxious for nothing, but in everything by prayer and supplication with thanksgiving let your requests be made known to God. And the peace of God, which surpasses all comprehension, shall guard you hearts and your minds in Christ Jesus."

ATTITUDE

Definition:

A position of the body or manner of carrying oneself: *stood in a graceful attitude*. Also, a state of mind or a feeling; disposition: *had a positive attitude about work*. It can also mean an arrogant or hostile state of mind or disposition.

Brief Explanation:

I have heard many parents state with dismay that they just did not know what to do with their adolescent because he or she had an attitude. By that, of course, they mean a negative, angry or hurtful attitude towards self, others or God. Usually, a negative attitude comes from negative thoughts and beliefs, which may come from having been hurt, rejected, abandoned or betrayed. Thus, when encountering someone with a primary negative attitude, it is important to take time to explore the possible reasons for the attitude. If hurt or rejection is evident (there are reasons for the attitude that are legitimate), then prayer for healing is needed and counsel to help them forgive (again, not always easy, taking time, sensitivity and grace, grace, grace) and accept God's view of the ones who have hurt or taken advantage of them. If however the attitude comes from rebellion or less legitimate reasons, repentance should be encouraged and renewing of the mind is necessary. Again, the word can be most powerful to help those with a half empty glass orientation to life, if they will submit themselves to the word of God.

The Word of God:
Ephesians 4:22-24

"...that, in reference to your former manner of life, you lay aside the old self, which is being corrupted in accordance with the lusts of deceit, and that you be renewed in the spirit of your mind and put on the new self, which in the likeness of God has been

created in righteousness and holiness of the truth."

Colossians 3:1-3, 15

"If then you have been raised up with Christ, keep seeking the things above where Christ is, seated at the right hand of God. Set your mind on the things above, not on the things that are on earth. For you have died, and your life is hidden with Christ in God. And let the peace of Christ rule in your hearts, to which indeed you were called in one body; and be thankful."

Hebrews 12: 1,2

" ...let us also lay aside every encumbrance and the sin which so easily entangles us, and let us run with endurance the race hat is set before us, fixing our eyes on Jesus."

BAD HABITS

Definition:

A bad habit is a recurrent, often unconscious pattern of behavior that is acquired through frequent repetition, or an established disposition of the mind or character. Also, bad habits may result from a customary manner or practice, which can become an addiction, especially to a mood altering drug.

Brief Explanation:

A bad habit is anything we do repeatedly that move us away from relationship with God or others. Habits are formed early in life, and most are benign, helpful, necessary for healthy living. Life would be most difficult if we had to actually think through how to eat or dress on a daily basis. What is presented here are negative or harmful habits, or perhaps irritating ones that we would like to change. Well, to change requires three primary steps. First, we must admit we need to make a change, and actually stop the habit. This is the easiest part of change, also the most difficult aspect to sustain. Secondly, and more importantly for long term change, we need to submit to a change of thinking. Our beliefs about the habit we have must be seen in light of truth, and we must no longer see our habit as a friend but something we really want out of our lives. Third, new behaviors designed to replace the old ones (usually necessary) we need then to practice, practice, practice.

Negative habits can be changed, if we want them to. It takes work, but God will help us. However, all techniques one might try will have greater impact with scripture and accountability.

For more on change, see *Journey to Wholeness by Dr. Stan DeKoven*

The Word of God:

Psalm 119:11

"Thy word I have treasured in my heart, That I may not sin against Thee."

James 4:7

"Submit therefore to God. Resist the devil and he will flee from You."

Matthew 7:7

"Ask and it shall be given to you, seek and you will find, knock and it will be opened to you."

John 14:15

"If you love me, you will keep my commandments."

1 Corinthians 15:33; 34

"Do not be deceived; Bad company corrupts good morals." Become sober-minded as you ought, and stop sinning; for some have no knowledge of God."

Ephesians 4:22-24

" ...in reference to your former manner of life, you lay aside the old self, which is being corrupted in accordance with the lusts of deceit, and that you be renewed in the spirit of your mind, and put on the new self, which in the likeness of God has been created in righteousness and holiness of the truth."

BEAUTY

Definition:

Beauty is the quality that gives pleasure to the mind or senses and is associated with such properties as harmony of form or color, excellence of artistry, truthfulness, and originality. A quality or feature that is most effective, gratifying, or telling.

Brief Explanation:

Vanity of vanities! All is vanity. (Ecc. 1:2) Well, this is certainly when it comes to holding on to or holding much hope for the perpetuation of beauty. In our narcissistic Western culture, the attempt to remain young, youthful, and ultimately beautiful has become a hopeless obsession. The reality is, we will all grow old (if we are blessed) and beauty will fade; thus, we would be wise to look at the beauty that is truly beautiful. A sunset, a smile of a child, the voice of a friend, the word of God, all are beautiful, and

Enjoying the beauty of God is important, and something to

encourage a struggler in life to consider.

The Word of God:

Philippians 4:8

"Finally, brethren, whatever is true, whatever is honorable, whatever is right, whatever is pure, whatever is lovely, whatever is of good repute, if there is any excellence and if anything worthy of praise, let your mind dwell on these things.

Psalms 27:4

"One thing I have asked from the Lord, that I shall seek: That I may dwell in the house of he Lord all the days of my life, To behold he beauty of the Lord, And to mediate in his temple."

Proverbs 31:30

"Charm is deceitful and beauty is vain, But a woman who fears the Lord, she shall be praised."

Isaiah 3:18

"In that day the Lord will take away the beauty of their anklets, headbands, crescent ornaments…"

BITTERNESS

Definition:

Bitterness is a feeling of deep and bitter anger and ill-will [syn: resentment, gall, rancor, rancour] It is a sharp and bitter manner [syn: acrimony, acerbity, jaundice]; the taste experience when quinine or coffee is taken into the mouth [syn: bitter]: the property of having a harsh unpleasant taste [syn: bitter]

Brief Explanation:

Over the years I have prayed with many men and women who had at the root of their depression and anxiety bitterness. Bitterness can so pollute the soul as to make one unable to develop healthy relationships with anyone. Resentment and unforgiveness often run parallel with bitterness, cocktail if swallowed which can destroy the heart of the one drinking, and hurt others near by. The only real hope for the bitter at heart is to face the truth of the bitterness, rather than blaming the one they are bitter against, and repent...beginning with forgiveness, a process more than event, but absolutely necessary for the release from the pain that bitterness can cause.

The Word of God:

Ephesians 4:31, 32

"Let all bitterness and wrath and anger and clamor and slander be put away from you, along with all malice. Be kind to one another, tender-hearted, forgiving each other, just as God in Christ also has forgiven you."

Hebrews 12:14, 15

"Pursue peace with all men and the sanctification without which no one will se the Lord. See to it that no one comes short of the grace of God; that no root of bitterness springing up causes trouble, and by it many be defiled."

Colossians 3:19

"Husbands, love your wives, and do not be embittered against them."

James 3:10-11; 14

*"From the same mouth come both blessing and cursing. My

brethren, these things ought not to be this way. Does a fountain send out from the same opening both fresh and bitter water? But if you have bitter jealousy and selfish ambition in your heat, do not be arrogant and so lie against the truth."

BORN AGAIN

Definition:

To be "born again means to be regenerated; renewed; having received spiritual life. It is a strictly biblical term, signifying moving from darkness to life through the knowledge of Jesus Christ.

Brief Explanation:

How could anyone deny the need for a savior? Similarly, how could anyone deny that Christ and his sacrifice is the greatest expression of love and mercy ever expressed? Well, many do, including many who seek help for what are essentially spiritual problems. In working with clients over the years, the greatest disappointment I have had has been to see men and women make emotional changes, yet never give their hearts to Christ. Their eternity, though they will face it better adjusted, is just as lost as one who never made changes to better their life. As a counselor, your hope is to lead many to Christ, but you must be sensitive to the timing of sharing your faith (a primary responsibility) and actually persuading them by your influence. It must be the clients' choice, and your prayer should be to have open hearts to share the love of Christ, leaving the results to the Lord. For more, see "*Bringing Heaven to Earth*" by Dr. Tim Dailey.

The Word of God:

John 3: 3

"Except a man be born again, he can not see the kingdom of God."

John 3:16

"For God so loved the world, that He gave His only begotten Son, that whoever believes in Him shall not perish, but have eternal life."

John 1:12, 13

"But as many as received Him, to them He gave the right to become children of God, even to those who believe in His name, who were born, not of blood nor of the will of the flesh nor of the will of man, but of God."

Romans 3:23

"For all have sinned and fall short of the glory of God."

Romans 6:23

"For the wages of sin is death, but the gift of God is eternal life in Christ Jesus our Lord."

Romans 8:1

"There is therefore now no condemnation for those who are in Christ Jesus."

Romans 10:9, 10

"If you confess with your mouth Jesus as Lord, and believe in your heart that God raised Him from the dead, you shall be saved; for with the heart man believes resulting in righteousness, and with the mouth he confesses, resulting in salvation."

CALLING

Definition:

The act of a person or thing that calls. Essentially for our study a call is a vocation, profession, or trade: What is your calling? It is also a summons: He had a calling to join the church; a strong impulse or inclination: She did it in response to an inner calling. For a believer, it is the call from something, to something, for something and about something…and the something all relates to God.

Brief Explanation:

For the believer, all of us have been called. It may not be to full-time paid preaching/teaching ministry in a church…but we are all called nonetheless. We were called out of darkness into his marvelous light…light is better. We have been called to his church, to be a member in koinonia or fellowship with Christ and one another. We have been called to be conformed to the very image of Christ, and we have been called to serve, according to the gifts and callings of God (more on this under stewardship of time and talent, and the section on Gifts). We all have a choice to do something with the call of God. We can accept or reject, embrace or neglect the call. But we cannot deny we are called for a purpose, as the scripture says.

The Word of God:

2 Timothy 2:19

"Nevertheless, the firm foundation of God stands, having this seal, "The Lord knows those who are His," and, "Let everyone who names the name of the Lord abstain from wickedness."

1 Peter 2: 5,9

"…you also, as living stones, are being built up as a spiritual house for a holy priesthood, to offer up spiritual sacrifices acceptable to God through Jesus Christ. But you are a chosen race, a royal priesthood, a holy nation, a people for God's own possession, that you may proclaim the excellencies of Him who has called your out of darkness into His marvelous light;"

Hebrews 10:25

"not forsaking our own assembling together, as is the habit of some, but encouraging one another; and all the more, as you see the day drawing near."

1 Corinthians 1:26

"For consider your calling, brethren, hat there were no many wise according to the flesh, not many mighty, not many noble; 27 but God has chosen the foolish things for the world to shame the wise, and God has chosen the weak things of the world to shame the things that are strong."

1 Thessalonians 4:7

"For God has not called us for the purpose of impurity, but in sanctification."

CHURCH

Definition:

> The church is defined as the groups of Christians who have their own beliefs and forms of worship [syn: Christian church] Also a place for public (especially Christian) worship; a service conducted in a church; "don't be late for church" and the body of people who attend or belong to a particular local church; "our church is hosting a picnic next week."

Brief Explanation:

Church life can be most satisfying and most disappointing,

depending on a number of factors. One thing is certain about the church; Jesus loves His church, is building it, and requires that his children not forsake it for something else. In my years as a therapist, I have had to recommend that people leave a certain congregation due to its abusive or neglectful practices, but that is very rare. IN most cases, people need to stay and work out their problems in the midst of the community of faith called the church, as it is a part of the over all healing process for most. Church, in spite of its inconsistencies, problems and weaknesses is God's instrument for us to work out character, try out friendships, make mistakes and hopefully learn grace, mercy and love; characteristics often missing in the dysfunctional family a counselee might have been raised in. I highly recommend the church. (* see *Building the Church God Wants and Supernatural Architecture by* Dr. Ken Chant and Dr. Stan DeKoven).

The Word of God:
Matthew 16:18

"And I also say to you that you are Peter, and upon this rock (revelation that Jesus is the Christ) I will build my church, and the gates of Hades shall not overpower it."

1Corinthians 14: 23

"If therefore the whole church should assemble together..."

2 Timothy 2:19

"Nevertheless, the firm foundation of God stands, having this seal, "The Lord knows those who are His," and, "Let everyone who names the name of the Lord abstain from wickedness."

1 Peter 2: 5,9

"...you also, as living stones, are being built up as a spiritual house for a holy priesthood, to offer up spiritual sacrifices acceptable to God through Jesus Christ. But you are a chosen race, a royal priesthood, a holy nation, a people for God's own possession, that you may proclaim the excellencies of Him who has called your out of darkness into His marvelous light;"

Hebrews 10:25

"...not forsaking our own assembling together, as is the habit of some, but encouraging one another; and all the more, as you see the day drawing near."

COMPASSION

Definition:

Deep awareness of the suffering of another coupled with the wish to relieve it.

Brief Explanation:

Compassion is love in action. Jesus was frequently moved with compassion on behalf of someone, releasing His power on behalf of another. It is still a key to the counseling process, and ministry in general. To be compassionate is to care deeply for another, communicated in empathy, warmth and respect, and which, unlike pity, shows the client that you care, and have every belief that with God and them, they can overcome.

The Word of God:

Matthew 9:36

"And seeing the multitudes, He felt compassion for them, because they were distressed and downcast like sheep without a shepherd.

Luke 7:13

"And when the Lord saw her, He felt compassion for her, and said to her. 'Do not weep.' "

Colossians 3:12

"And so, as those who have been chosen of God, holy and beloved, put on a heart of compassion, kindness, humility, gentleness and patience…"

1Peter 3:8

"To sum it up, let all be harmonious, sympathetic, brotherly, kindhearted and humble in spirit."

James 1:27

"This is pure and undefiled religion in the sight of our God and Father, to visit orphans and widows in their distress, and to keep oneself unstained by the world."

CONCEIT

Definition:

Conceit is a favorable and especially unduly high opinion of one's own abilities or worth; thinking more of oneself than deserved.

Brief Explanation:

I heard someone say "conceit is a fault, and I have none." Well, that is probably beyond conceit, and into the land of delusion. Conceit is akin to denial, that is, it is a braggadocios attitude that states "I am better than others, or my problems are less than others." In fact, there is always someone better, smarter, faster, better looking than us, if only in the eye of the beholder. Thus, conceit is a wrong self-appraisal, and indicated insecurity to the highest degree.

When faced with a person filled with themselves, it is difficult to help them until they are willing to see themselves in light of the word of God. Helping a person accept both strengths and weakness, and our common need for God's grace is a gift, but one that a truly narcissistic, conceited person is not likely to benefit from.

The Word of God:

Proverbs 16:18, 19

"Pride goes before destruction, And a haughty spirit before stumbling. It is better to be of a humble spirit with the lowly, Than to divide the spoil with the proud."

1 John 2:16

"For all that is in the world, the lust of the flesh and the lust of the eyes and the boastful pride of life, is not from the Father, but is from the world."

2 Samuel 18:18

"Now Absalom in his lifetime had taken and set up for himself a pillar which is in the King's Valley, for he said "I have no son to preserve my name." So he named the pillar after his own name, and it is called Absalom's Monument to this day.

For more, see "Pride."

CONFESSION

Definition:

Confession is defined as the act or process of confessing. It is something confessed, especially disclosure of one's sins to a priest for absolution. A confession can also be a written or oral statement acknowledging guilt, made by one who has been accused or charged with an offense. From a Christian view it is an avowal of belief in the doctrines of a particular faith; a creed. Also, a church or group of worshipers adhering to a specific creed.

Brief Explanation:

In James 5:16, reference below, the writer provides a basis for much of talk counseling from a Christian perspective. Confession means to tell the story (hopefully truthfully) with a focus of learning the areas where sin or wrong decisions have led one in the wrong direction, so they can in turn repent (turn around, correct ones thinking to line up with the truth of God's word) and receive the healing that the Lord has. To hear another person's story is a great privilege, not to be taken lightly. As a person opens their heart, the counselor must also open their hearts with a willingness to share hurts or problems that are similar to the person confessing. Of course, wisdom is needed. That is, we never confess to the person seeking help things in our lives that are active problems, but ones we have, by God's grace, overcome. Confession is good for the soul, if it is truthful, and is then confronted in love by the word of God. Encourage confession, not gossip, as confession deals with me and my responsibility, not them and theirs. see *Mountain Movers* by Dr. Ken Chant.

The Word of God:

Psalm 32:5

"I acknowledged my sin to Thee, And my iniquity I did not hide; I said, "I will confess my transgressions to the Lord"; And Thou didst forgive the guilt of my sin."

1 John 1:9

"If we confess our sins, He is faithful and righteous to forgive us our sins and to cleanse us from all unrighteousness."

James 5:16

"Therefore, confess your sins to one another, and pray for one another, so that you may be healed. The effective prayer of a righteous man can accomplish much."

CONFIDENCE

Definition:

Confidence is a trust or faith in a person or thing. It can include a trusting relationship: *I took them into my confidence.* It can also be seen as a feeling of assurance that a confidant will keep a secret: *I am telling you this in strict confidence.* Also, feeling of assurance, especially of self-assurance.

Brief Explanation:

Confidence in your skill and spiritual maturity is necessary for a person in need to receive genuine counsel and help. If there is a lack of confidence, the person questioning your motives or expertise, it will be most difficult to make positive impact on their lives. Our confidence is in God, his word and grace, along with our skills as humans and counselors. A combination of training[1] and the empowerment of the Holy Spirit is needed to be an effective caregiver.

The Word of God:

---

[1] If training is needed, we recommend the counselor training program offered by Vision International University, www.vision.edu.

Proverbs 3:26

"For the Lord will be your confidence, And will keep your foot from being caught."

Psalm 118:8, 9

"It is better to take refuge in the Lord Than to trust in man. It is better to take refuge in the Lord Than to trust in princes."

Psalm 71:5

"For Thou are my hope; O Lord God, Thou are my confidence from my youth.

Proverbs 14:26

"In the fear of the Lord there is strong confidence, and his children will have refuge."

1 John 3:21

"Beloved, if our heart does not condemn us, we have confidence before God;"

1 John 5:14, 15

"And this is the confidence which we have before Him, that, if we ask anything according to His will, He hears us."

CONFORMITY

Definition:

Conformity is defined as similarity in form or character; agreement: *I acted in conformity with my principles.* Further, it is an action or behavior in correspondence with socially accepted standards, conventions, rules, or laws: *conformity to university regulations.*

Brief Explanation:

It is only natural to want to fit in. This is true with children, adolescents and adults, in and out of church. In adolescence, we call this peer pressure, and subtle or not so subtle pressure to be like everyone else is evident amongst teens. But the peer pressure thing continues throughout life (just see how different folks dress in various churches and what happens in reaction when someone looks different). Of course, we are to be conformed to something, the image of Christ. That is, we need to allow the Holy Spirit to work His work in us, producing the fruit of the Holy Spirit or Godly character in us. We want that kind of conformity, while allowing for individual differences that might be unpleasant to us, but are not in conflict with God's word.

The Word of God:

Romans 12:1,2

"I urge you therefore, brethren, by the mercies of God, to present our bodies a living and holy sacrifice, acceptable to God, which is your spiritual service of worship. And do not be conformed to this world, but be transformed by the renewing of your mind, that you may prove what the will of God is, that which is good and acceptable and perfect."

2 Corinthians 6:14, 17, 18

"Do not be bound together with unbelievers; for what partnership has righteousness and lawlessness, or what fellowship has light with darkness? "Therefore, come out from their midst and be separate," says the Lord. "And do not touch what is unclean; and I will welcome you. And I will be a father to you. And you shall be sons and daughters to Me," Says the Lord Almighty."

COURAGE

Definition:

The state or quality of mind or spirit that enables one to face danger, fear, or vicissitudes with self-possession, confidence, and resolution; bravery.

Brief Explanation:

I loved both the movies Brave heart and Norma Rae. Both speak of courage, expressed differently, as the key characters faced great odds and overcame in different ways. Courage to face the truth, to deal with problems, to make new choices comes from the heart, especially when the heart has been changed by God's power. As a counselor, it is essential to encourage (a form of courage) your counselee to take courage, trusting that the Lord will help them wherever they find themselves. See *Faith Dynamics* by Dr. Ken Chant.

The Word of God:

Deuteronomy 31:6

"Be strong and courageous, do not be afraid or tremble at them, for the Lord you God is the one who goes with you. He will not fail your or forsake you."

2 Chronicles 15:7

"But you, be strong and do not lose courage, for there is reward for your work."

Psalms 27: 14

"Wait for the Lord; be strong, and let your heart take courage; yes, wait for the Lord."

John 16:33

"These things have spoken to you, that in Me you may have peace. In the world you have tribulation, but take courage; I have overcome the world."

DEATH

Definition:

Death is the enemy of life. It is defined as the act of dying; termination of life. Further, it is the state of being dead.

Brief Explanation:

Issues of death and dying will frequently come up in counseling. Being aware of the common reactions people may have during the dying process and for the bereaved after the loss of a loved one is essential to good counsel and care in general.

Grieving is often misunderstood. It is thoroughly biblical and healthy to grieve, mourn, but if believers, not without hope. That is, we grieve our loss (blessed are those who mourn, for they shall be comforted) but with the knowledge that to be absent in the body is to be present in the Lord. Glib "he or she is in a better place" or "God needed your mom or dad more than you" can be cruel, and are to be avoided. The ministry of presence, listening, empathetically, is the best medicine for one in times of grief. Of course, watch for delayed responses, sometimes years later of unresolved grief. See *Grief Relief* by Dr. Stan DeKoven.

The Word of God:

Psalm 116:15

"Precious in the sight of the Lord Is the death of His godly ones."

Psalm 23:4

"Even though I walk through the valley of the shadow of death, I fear no evil; for Thou art with me; Thy rod and Thy staff, they comfort me."

Romans 6:23

"For the wages of sin is death, but the free gift of God is eternal life in Christ Jesus our Lord."

John 11:25,26

"Jesus said to her, "I am the resurrection and the life; he who believes in Me shall live even if he dies, and everyone who lives and believes in Me shall never die. Do you believe this?"

Hebrews 9:27,28

"And inasmuch as it is appointed for men to die once and after this comes judgment, so Christ also, having been offered once to bear the sins of many, shall appear a second time for salvation without reference to sin, to those who eagerly await Him."

1 Thessalonians 4:14

"For if believe that Jesus died and rose again, even so God will bring with Him those who have fallen asleep in Jesus."

1 John 3:2

"Beloved, now we are children of God, and it has not appeared as yet what we shall be. We know that, when he appears, we shall be like Him, because we shall see Him just as He is."

Revelation 21:4

"...and He shall wipe away every tear from their eyes; and

there shall no longer be any death; there shall no longer be any mourning, or crying, or pain; the first things have passed away."

1 Corinthians 15:55-57

"O death, where is your victory? O death, where is your sting?" The sting of death is sin, and the power of sin is the law; but thanks be to God, who gives us the victory through our Lord Jesus Christ."

DEFEAT

Definition:

Defeat is defined as the act of defeating or state of being defeated; failure to win. Also seen as a coming to naught of a thing, or frustration, such as the defeat of a life long dream.

Brief Explanation:

"I can't" or "yes but," frequent phrases heard by counselors are difficult to deal with, and are often experienced as forms of resistance to the counseling process. A defeated person, one who feels they cannot change, cannot overcome, cannot make it, are not good enough, etc., are some of the most difficult cases we deal with.

Encouraging them to overcome is often the best we can offer. Part of a counselors hope is to give the word and words of wisdom that counteract the negative defeatist attitudes of the client. Taking thoughts captive (cognitive restructuring or renewing the mind) is key, and is hard work, that you hope the client will engage in. God's word, the seed of life is significantly more powerful than any word sown by others of a negative bent, and we must trust that over time the good seed will overtake the negative, and defeat will turn into victory.

The Word of God:

Proverbs 24:16

"For a righteous man falls seven times, and rises again, But the wicked stumble in time of calamity."

Proverbs 24:16

"For a righteous man falls seven times, and rises again, But the wicked stumble in time of calamity."

2 Corinthians 12:9

"And He has said to me, "My grace is sufficient for you, for power is perfected in weakness." Most gladly, therefore, I will rather boast about my weaknesses, that the power of Christ may dwell in me."

DECISIONS

Definition:

> The act or process of deciding; determination, as of a question or doubt, by making a judgment: They must make a decision between these two contestants. Further, it is the act of or need for making up one's mind: This is a difficult decision. A decision is something that is decided; resolution: He made a poor decision or a judgment formally pronounced by a court.

Brief Explanation:

Someone asked the question, which is worse, ignorance or apathy; the answer, I don't know and I don't care. Well, sometimes making a decision, even an important one can be made worse due to lack of information (as to which course of action is best) or a lack of caring, or sometimes fear and lack of experience lead to difficulty in making a necessary decision.

Of course, we do make decisions every day of our life. To get up, go to work, pray, not pray, are all decisions. When decision making is critical, however, is when the consequences of a decision might be problematic (to marry or not to marry, to quite a job and seek another, etc.). This is where wisdom, council, research and common sense become important. The word of God provides guidance for us, but rarely specific answers (except things like should I steal that candy bar...the answer is obvious, no additional guidance is needed). Thus, we need to know the principles of the Word of God, use the good brain God has given us, seek wise counsel, and make the most informed decision possible given the information we have...and trust God.

The Word of God:

Proverbs 3:3, 6

"Trust in the Lord with all your heart, and do not lean on your own understanding; in all your ways acknowledge him, and he will direct your path."

Proverbs 16:33

"The lot is cast into the lap, but its every decision is from the Lord."

Joel 3:14

" Multitudes, multitudes in the valley of decision! For the day of the Lord is near in the valley of decision."

2 Corinthians 4:16

"Therefore we do not lose heart, but though our outer man is decaying, yet our inner man is being renewed day by day."

DEMONS

Definition:

Demons are defined as evil, supernatural beings; workers of the devil. It can also be seen as a persistently tormenting person, force, or passion: *the demon of drug addiction.*

Brief Explanation:

I am not a demon chaser, though I have found that they will occasionally show up in the counseling process. Evil does exist, and demonization is a real problem for some. The divine ability to discern if a demon is present in the life of the client is important, as many times it is most difficult to tell if a symptom presented is psychological or spiritual. If you try to cast a demon out of a person who is suffering with a personality disorder, it will not work, and will often cause damage to the precious person. Thus, it is wise to seek a second opinion, from a pastor or other professional who has experience in this field. I know, the client wants relief today, but they can frequently wait until you have properly assessed if the problem is indeed demonic. If it is, it is best to work in a team. You must recognize your authority in Christ, and minister with the empowerment of the Holy Spirit.

The Word of God:

Mark 16:17, 18

"And these signs swill accompany those who have believed: in My name hey will cast out demons..."

1John 3:8

"The one who practices sin is of the devil; for the devil has sinned from the beginning. The son of God appeared for this purpose, that He might destroy the works of the devil."

James 4:7

"Submit therefore to God. Resist the devil and he will flee from you."

DEPRESSION

Definition:

Depression is the condition of feeling sad or despondent. From a psychological view it is a mental disorder characterized by an inability to concentrate, insomnia, loss of appetite, feelings of extreme sadness, guilt, helplessness and hopelessness, and thoughts of death. Also called clinical depression.

Brief Explanation:

There can be multiple reasons for depression. Sadly, many of God's people suffer from the overwhelming sadness and lethargy caused by depression. It is important for a counselor to determine the root cause of the depression where possible. Is it a delayed grief response? If so, grief is the answer. Is it a problem with brain chemistry? Then medication and prayer for healing is key. Is it unresolved hurt? Issues of abandonment or betrayal, bitterness and unforgiveness? Then confession and repentance is needed for victory. But we must acknowledge that it can be a combination of any and all of this, or more. Thus, to counsel someone suffering may require a multidisciplinary approach, where you first rule out the physical (a good physical may help, as may medication), while encouraging the client to share their story. Often, a local support group such as a home fellowship can help, along with light physical exercise, which can counteract mild symptoms of depression. Depression, a major problem in Western culture is in the church as the church is a microcosm of the world in which we live. See *Dazzling Secrets for Despondent Saints,* Dr. Ken Chant.

The Word of God:

1 John 4:4

"You are from God, little children, and have overcome them; because greater is He who is in you than he who is in the world."

Psalm 42:11

"Why are you in despair, O my soul? And why have you become disturbed within me? Hope in God, for I shall yet praise Him, The help of my countenance, and my God."

Isaiah 26:3

"The steadfast of mind Thou wilt keep in perfect peace, Because he trusts in Thee."

Isaiah 40:29

"He gives strength to the weary, And to him who lacks might He increases power."

Isaiah 53:4,5

"Surely our grief He Himself bore, And our sorrows He carried; Yet we ourselves esteemed Him stricken, Smitten of God, and afflicted. But He was pierced through for our transgressions, He was crushed for our iniquities; The chastening for our well-being fell upon Him, And by His scourging we are healed."

Nehemiah 8:10

"Then he said to them, "Go, eat of the fat, drink of the sweet, and send portions to him who had nothing prepared; for this day is holy to our Lord. Do not be grieved, for the joy of the Lord is your strength."

John 14:27

"Peace I leave with you; My peace I give to you; not as the world gives, do I give to you. Let not your heart be troubled, nor let it be fearful."

DISCOURAGEMENT

Definition:

Discouragement is the feeling of despair in the face of obstacles [syn: disheartenment, dismay]; the expression of opposition and disapproval [ant: encouragement]; the act of discouraging something from happening.

Brief Explanation:

Often discouragement can manifest as a mild form of depression. Fortunately, it is usually not as deep a problem as depression, but is nonetheless one that will be frequently seen in church life. The counter measure for discouragement is encouragement and with that a dose of courage to act.

Discouragement can usually be linked to negative thinking about oneself and the circumstances they are facing. Thus, helping the client seek and find the truth from God's perspective (yes, you many have failed, lost, did not get what you hoped for, etc.) which is that we are blessed, precious, and ultimately worthwhile, and with new skills and assistance we can face life with courage. Also see Dazzling Secrets for Despondent Saints, by Dr. Ken Chant.

The Word of God:

Psalm 147:3

"He heals the brokenhearted and binds up their wounds."

2 Corinthians 4:8, 14

"We are afflicted in every way, but not crushed; perplexed, but not despairing... knowing that He who raised the Lord Jesus will raise us also with Jesus and will present us with you."

Proverbs 17:22

"A joyful heart is good medicine, But a broken spirit dries up the bones."

Psalm 51:17

"The sacrifices of God are a broken spirit; A broken and a contrite heart, O God, You will not despise."

DIVORCE

Definition:

To divorce is to dissolve the marriage bond between a man and wife. It means to end marriage with (one's spouse) by way of legal divorce.

Brief Explanation:

For many generations, divorce was seen as the unforgivable sin. With divorce rates consistently hovering around the 50% mark, it has moved from unforgivable to an epidemic that must be addressed in the life of the church. Thus, many churches are realizing their responsibility to help people who have experienced the pain of divorce, or who are facing the present abandonment of a spouse or parent.

The helping process is similar to that of working with a loss due to death. The primary difference is that the corpse, so to speak, is still walking around. Thus, it is in many ways more difficult to come to a place of acceptance, learning from mistakes made, repenting for areas of sin, and gaining a new perspective before venturing again if at all into the land of matrimony. See *To the Corinthians* by Dr. Ken Chant for an excellent theological and practical discussion on the divorce and remarriage issue, and *Marriage and Family Life*, previously referenced.

The Word of God:

Genesis 2:24

"For this reason a man shall leave his father and his mother, and be joined to his wife; and they shall become one flesh."

Matthew 5:31, 32

"It was said, Whoever sends his wife away, let him give her a certificate of divorce; but I say to you that everyone who divorces his wife, except for the reason of unchastity, makes her commit adultery; and whoever marries a divorced woman commits adultery."

Mark 10:11, 12

"And He said to them, Whoever divorces his wife and marries another woman commits adultery against her; and if she herself divorces her husband and marries another man, she is committing adultery."

1 Corinthians 7:10, 11

"But to the married I give instructions, not I, but the Lord, that the wife should not leave her husband (but if she does leave, she must remain unmarried, or else be reconciled to her husband), and that the husband should not divorce his wife."

DOUBT

Definition:

Doubt means to be undecided or skeptical about something. Further, to tend to disbelieve; distrust; to regard as unlikely: *I doubt that we'll arrive on time.*

Brief Explanation:

I don't doubt that doubt is a major problem for counselors. First, often we doubt that a client will actually change, the client doubts our ability, and we all doubt at times God's care for us. But doubt is a real issue in counseling, and must be faced openly, and with faith. The development of trust, a key to our growth as humans (See Bohac and DeKoven, *Human Development*) is essential in counseling. Thus, I find it helpful to deal with the doubts of clients directly and with gentleness and care. Doubt is especially heard when loss has come, loss of a loved one or situation like a job. It is hard to hear a believer share genuine doubts, but they are a part of faith, a faith that as a counselor we have the honor to grapple with, with our client.

The Word of God:

Hebrews 11:6

"And without faith it is impossible to please Him, for he who comes to God must believe that He is and that He is a rewarder of those who seek Him."

James 1:5-7

"But if any of you lacks wisdom, let him ask of God, who gives to all generously and without reproach, and it will be given to him. But he must ask in faith without any doubting, for the one who

doubts is like the surf of the sea, driven and tossed by the wind. For that man ought not to expect that he will receive anything from the Lord."

Hebrews 12:1, 2

"Therefore, since we have so great a cloud of witnesses surrounding us, let us also lay aside every encumbrance and the sin which so easily entangles us, and let us run with endurance the race that is set before us, fixing our eyes on Jesus, the author and perfecter of faith, who for the joy set before Him endured the cross, despising the shame, and has sat down at the right hand of the throne of God."

DRUG ABUSE

Definition:

Drug abuse is a habitual use of drugs to alter one's mood, emotion, or state of consciousness.

Brief Explanation:

Unlike alcohol, non pharmaceutical drug use is clearly forbidden in scripture, both the use and abuse. When drugs become a problem, help is readily available. Of course, though help is readily available, often it is not availed of due to the defense mechanism known as denial. Like the alcoholic, the drug abuser denies the need for help.

Drug abuse does not only affect the health of the person abusing the substance, but also the family and friends. It is an insidious problem, yet God can heal. All members of the family will need help, support and strength, but families who deal with the denial, confront the abuser and if the abuser receives help, healthy family life is more than possible. For more, see the books * *Addictions Counseling and 12 Steps to Wholeness* by Dr Stan DeKoven

The Word of God:

2 Timothy 1:7

"For God has not given us a spirit of timidity, but of power and love and discipline."

James 1:14, 15

"But each one is tempted when he is carried away and enticed by his own lust. Then when lust has conceived, it gives birth to sin; and when sin is accomplished, it brings forth death."

ENEMIES

Definition:

One who feels hatred toward, intends injury to, or opposes the interests of another is an enemy; a foe. It can also be seen as a hostile power or force, such as a nation.

Brief Explanation:

Unfortunately, many people will have as a part of their presenting problem hurts and wounds caused by significant others in their past. Some of the people can be classified as enemies, at least in the mind of the client seeking help. Whether real or from a paranoiac ideation (paranoid thoughts), an enemy in the mind must be addressed if counseling is going to be successful.

One primary reason many will hold on to anger and bitterness towards a perceived enemy is the fear that the enemy will hurt them (again). To forgive does not require trust in anyone other than God, but is essential, and the focus of counseling after trust with you has been established.

The Word of God:
Romans 12:17-19

"Never pay back evil for evil to anyone. Respect what is right in the sight of all men. If possible, so far as it depends on you, be at peace with all men. Never take you own revenge beloved, but leave room for the wrath of God, for it is written, "Vengeance is Mine, I will repay," says the Lord."

Matthew 5:43, 44

"You have heard that it was said, "You shall love your neighbor and hat your enemy. But I say to you, love your enemies and pray for those who persecute you."

Matthew 18:21, 22

"Then Peter came and said to Him, "Lord, how often shall my brother sin against me and I forgive him? Up to seven times?" Jesus said to him, "I do not say to you, up tot seven times, but up to seventy times seven."

Psalm 97:10

"Hate evil, you who love the Lord, who preserves the souls of His godly ones; He delivers them from the hand of the wicked."

ENVY/JEALOUSY

Definition:

Envy is a feeling of resentful discontent, begrudging admiration, or covetousness with regard to another's advantage, possessions, or attainments. Jealousy is similar, being rooted in fear that someone else has something that they deserve.

Brief Explanation:

Many couples suffer from envy and jealousy of each other. Pastors and other spiritual leaders can often be jealous of a colleague, thinking that somehow they are being cheated by the success of another. Much of envy and jealously is rooted in an unhealthy appraisal of oneself, actually believing that one deserves things not earned. Further, it can be rooted in fear...of being cheated and not properly cared for. Envy and jealousy is like a cancer, eating away at the person's proper perspective on life and circumstances.

In dealing with envy and jealousy, using the concept of mirroring can be helpful (see Dr. Richard Walters' book; Hand to Hand). To mirror is to reflect the statements and feelings of the person (such as "Why does she get to stay home; why does he get to see his friends; etc.) at a feeling and meaning level (you think it is unfair that they...). Mirroring will often help the honest person eventually see the anger, fear, self-centeredness, etc. that is at the root of the envy and jealousy, and will help you to help them see and eventually repent of this insidious area of sin and dysfunction.

Of course, not all jealousy is bad, as seen in God being a jealous God and Paul who jealously guarded the church against wrong teaching.

The Word of God:

Proverbs 6:34

"For jealously enrages a man, and he will not spare in the day of vengeance. He will not accept any ransom nor will he be content though you give many gifts."

Proverbs 23:17

"Do not let your heart envy sinners, but live in the fear of the Lord always."

Matthew 27:18

"For he (Jesus) knew that because of envy they had delivered Him up."

James 3:14

"But if you have bitter jealousy and selfish ambition in your heart, do not be arrogant and so lie against the truth."

2 Corinthians 11:2

"For I am jealous for you with a godly jealousy; for I betrothed you to one husband, that to Christ I might present you as a pure virgin."

FAITH

Definition:

Faith is a confident belief in the truth, value, or trustworthiness of a person, idea, or thing. It is a belief that does not rest on logical proof or material evidence. Faith can be seen in loyalty to a person or thing; allegiance: *keeping faith with one's supporters.* In <u>Christianity;</u> the theological virtue defined as secure belief in God and a trusting acceptance of God's will.

Brief Explanation:

Faith is basic trust that something will actually happen. Most clients come for counseling with wishes and expectations, often unreasonable, that the anointed, gifted, practically infallible counselor will have all answers and wisdom. Of course, it is not long before they are disappointed, as reality sets in. Yet, a certain amount of reasonable faith is needed, in the Lord, the counselor and the process if effective help is to be given. In the beginning, it may well be necessary for the counselor to have significantly more faith in both the process and the Lord than the client, but this is fine until trust (a component of faith) is established. Rest assured, without faith it is impossible to please the Lord and accomplish much. But with faith in God, all things are possible. See both *Faith Dynamics* and *Mountain Movers* by Dr. Ken Chant)

The Word of God:

Hebrews 11:1

"Now faith is the assurance of things hoped for, the conviction of things not seen."

Hebrews 11:6

"And without faith it is impossible to please Him, for he who comes to God must believe that He is and that He is a rewarder of those who seek Him."

Romans 10:17

"So faith comes from hearing, and hearing by the word of Christ."

Ephesians 2:8, 9

"For by grace you have been saved through faith; and not of yourselves, it is the gift of God; not as a result of works, so that no one may boast."

Romans 14:23

"But he who doubts is condemned if he eats, because his eating is not from faith, and whatever is not from faith is sin."

FEAR

Definition:

Fear is defined as a feeling of agitation and anxiety caused by the presence or imminence of danger. Further, it is a state or condition marked by this feeling: *living in fear.* Also, a feeling of disquiet or apprehension: *a fear of looking foolish.* In a more positive sense, it is an extreme reverence or awe, as toward a supreme power (God).

Brief Explanation:

Fear is similar to anxiety, experienced by most as psychological pain or dread. It is often expressed in symptoms such as a panic response (shortness of breath, fear that one is having a heart attack, etc.) or a phobia (focused fear, like that of heights, flying, etc.) to such an extent that it is debilitating to the client. As noted, there are many different expressions of fear, from a sense of dread to debilitating phobias or panic responses. The root of fear is generally a wrong interpretation of thoughts that bombard the mind of the person. Taking authority over ones thoughts is the goal, conforming the thoughts to God's word the key; but again, as with many areas of difficulty, this is easier said than done.

For those with minor fears, simply talking about the problems one is facing can help, as can prayer for God's intervention. Often confronting the negative beliefs that are inevitably a part of the fear can help.

Where the problem is more insidious, cognitive psychology can be an effective tool in helping someone with overwhelming anxiety, and professional help may be required. God is certainly able to help someone with overwhelming fears, and his word, meditated upon consistently can make a major and dramatic difference for many.

The Word of God:

Psalm 34:4

"I sought the Lord, and He answered me, and delivered me from all my fears."

John 14:27

"Peace I leave with you; My peace I give to you; not as the world gives do I give to you. Do not let your heart be troubled, nor let it be fearful."

Isaiah 41:10

"Do not fear, for I am with you; do not anxiously look about you, for I am your God. I will strengthen you, surely I will help you, surely I will uphold you with My righteous right hand."

Philippians 4:6, 7

"Be anxious for nothing, but in everything by prayer and supplication with thanksgiving let your requests be made known to God."

Hebrews 13:5, 6

"Make sure that your character is free from the love of money, being content with what you have; for He Himself has said, "I will never desert you, nor will I ever forsake you," so that we confidently say, "The Lord is my helper, I will not be afraid, what will man do to me?"

FORGIVENESS

Definition:

The act of forgiving; pardon; to remit or cancel.

Brief Explanation:

It has been said, to err is human, to forgive divine...and difficult for many. This is especially true for people who have been deeply hurt through rejection, abandonment or betrayal, the results of abuse and neglect. Forgiveness is a process, beginning for most with an act of obedience (as Christ commands, that if we are going to be forgiven, we must forgive). It follows with identifying who is responsible for the offense; this may take time and patience, as often the offense is perceived, often real, often mixed. Once the responsible party is determined, judgment of the offense is to be made, and then statements of relief or forgiveness, undeserved though it may be, are to be done.

Again, this is process not an event, and several experiential exercises can be used to help facilitate the process, from role play to empty chair (imagining the person who offended in the chair), speaking to them ones hurt, then taking the "persons place to respond", with a hope that empathy and clarity of thought will ensue, to letter writing (don't mail them) The act of externalization is often highly therapeutic. Whatever technique is used, the goal is the same, to bring about genuine and heart felt forgiveness, which frees the client to use health energy for growth and change.

The Word of God:

Psalm 32:1, 2

"How blessed is he whose transgression is forgiven, whose sin is covered! How blessed is the man to whom the Lord does not impute iniquity, and in whose spirit there is no deceit!"

Psalm 51:1, 2

"Be gracious to me, O God, according to Your loving kindness;

according to the greatness of Your compassion blot out my transgressions. Wash me thoroughly from my iniquity and cleanse me from my sin."

Isaiah 43:25

"I, even I, am the one who wipes out your transgressions for My own sake, and I will not remember your sins."

Psalm 103:2-5

"Bless the Lord, O my soul, and forget none of His benefits; who pardons all your iniquities, who heals all your diseases; who redeems your life from the pit, who crowns you with lovingkindness and compassion; who satisfies your years with good things, so that your youth is renewed like the eagle."

Matthew 5:7

"Blessed are the merciful, for they shall receive mercy."

Mark 11:25, 26

"Whenever you stand praying forgive, if you have anything against anyone, so that your Father who is in heaven will also forgive you your transgressions. But if you do not forgive, neither will your Father who is in heaven forgive your transgressions."

Proverbs 25:21, 22

"If your enemy is hungry, give him food to eat; and if he is thirsty, give him water to drink. For you will heap burning coals on his head, and the Lord will reward you."

Matthew. 5:23, 24

"If therefore you are presenting your offering at the alter, and there remember that your brother has something against you, leave your offering there before the altar, and go your way; first be reconciled to your brother, and then come and present your *offering."*

Ephesians 4:32

"Be kind to one another, tender-hearted, forgiving each other, just as God in Christ also has forgiven you."

FRIENDS

Definition:

A friend is a person whom one knows, likes, and trusts. It is also an acquaintance. Further, it can be a person with whom one is allied in a struggle or cause; a comrade.

Brief Explanation:

Making friends is fairly natural for most children as they grow up. However, developing true, close and intimate relationships is not always easy in the body of Christ. There are many reasons that can be proposed for this reality, but regardless ones opinion, finding friends is an art form, requiring that the person needing friends be friendly. A counselor can model friendship, but can rarely be the friend of the client, due to the relationship dynamics of counselor/counselee. The church can and of course should be a place where friendships, based upon a common faith in Jesus Christ are developed. A counselor needs to encourage friendship development, both in the church and community.

The Word of God:

Proverbs 17:17

"A friend loves as all times, and a brother is born for adversity."

Amos 3:3

"Do two men walk together unless they have made an appointment?"

Galatians 6:2

"Bear one another's burdens, and thereby fulfill the law of Christ."

Proverbs 27:6

"Faithful are the wounds of a friend, but deceitful are the kisses of an enemy."

Proverbs 17:9

"He who conceals a transgression seeks love, But he who Repeats a matter separates intimate friends."

Ecclesiastes 4:9, 10

"Two are better than one because they have a good return for their labor. For if either of them falls, the one will lift up his companion. But woe to the one who falls when there is not another to lift him up."

Romans 12:15

"Rejoice with those who rejoice, and weep with those who weep."

Proverbs 13:20

"He who walks with wise men will be wise, but the companion of fools will suffer harm."

Proverbs 27:10

"Do not forsake your own friend or your father's friend, and do not go to your brother's house in the day of your calamity; better is a neighbor who is near than a brother far away."

FUTURE

Definition:

The future is the indefinite time yet to come. It is something that will happen in time to come. Further, it can be seen as a prospective or expected condition, especially one considered with regard to growth, advancement, or development.

Brief Explanation:

Often to move into a future and a hope requires dealing with the past. Grieving losses, resolving conflict, forgiving, etc. are often the weights that beset us, or hold us back from our future destiny.

To look to the future, a time when life is problem free is a fantasy we cannot afford to buy into. However, a future with purpose and meaning is quite possible for the most difficult of cases, for we are blessed in Christ and have hope in him. Coming along side a client, speaking future into them in keeping with their gifts and abilities is something a counselor can do by God's grace.

The Word of God:

Proverbs 3:1, 2

"My son, do not forget my teaching, but let your heart keep my commandments; for length of days and years of life and peace they will add to you."

1 John 2:17

"The world is passing away, and also its lusts; but the one who does the will of God lives forever."

Proverbs 16:9

"The mind of man plans his way, but the Lord directs his

steps."

Proverbs 16:3

"Commit your works to the Lord and your plans will be established."

Mark 9:23

"And Jesus said to him, "If You can? All things are possible to him who believes."

Proverbs 15:22

"Without consultation, plans are frustrated, but with many counselors they succeed."

Jeremiah 29:11

"For I know the plans that I have for you, declares the Lord, plans for welfare and not for calamity to give you a future and a hope."

John 14:2, 3

"In My Father's house are many dwelling places; if it were not so, I would have told you; for I go to prepare a place for you. If I go and prepare a place for you, I will come again and receive you to myself, that where I am, there you may be also".

GIFTS FROM GOD

Definition (Gifts):

A gift or gifts are something that is bestowed voluntarily and without compensation. It is the act, right, or power of giving. Gifts are also talents, endowments, aptitudes, or inclinations of a positive and beneficial nature.

Brief Explanation:

Many people coming for counseling are unable to identify the gifts they have received from the Lord, whether natural or spiritual. In fact, all people are gifted in one way or another, and their very gifts can be strengths to help them in their time of trouble. Encouraging them to identify or helping them identify and use their gifts for problem solving or to serve others can be highly therapeutic.

The Word of God:

Acts 2:38

"Repent and let each of you be baptized in the name of Jesus Christ for the forgiveness of your sins, and you will receive the gift of the Holy Spirit."

Romans 1:11

"For I long to see you in order that I may impart some spiritual gift to you, that you may be established, that is that I may be encouraged together with you while among you, each of us by the others faith, both yours and mine."

Romans 6:23

"For the wages of sin is death, but the free gift of God is eternal life in Christ Jesus our Lord."

Romans 12: 6

"And since we have gifts that differ according to the grace given to us, let ach exercise them accordingly; if prophecy according to the proportion of his faith..."

1 Corinthians 12:31

"And there are varieties of effects (gifts), but the same God

who works all things in all persons."

James 1:17

"Every good thing bestowed and every perfect gift is from above, coming down from the Father of lights, with whom there is no variation or shifting shadow."

GIVING

Definition:

Giving is defined as making a present of something to someone. Of providing something to another of value to the person for the benefit of another. This is just a summary of giving, which can be used in many contexts.

Brief Explanation:

As you can readily see from the definition above, the word giving has many meanings, and can be used in many contexts. Many people come to counseling due to, in their estimation, giving too much, as in the case of a co-dependent. Of course, they cannot see that their giving is to get, not truly as altruistic as they assume. Many are not used to giving at all, but to receiving; love, forgiveness, support, etc. They have never learned to actually give to benefit others; one of the reasons for their condition. Giving was an important issue to Jesus, as he stated that the condition of the heart/mind was measured by ones generosity (where your treasure is, i.e., time, talent and treasure, there is your heart also). Often Christians can be the least giving of all cultural groups, and knowing the giving nature of a person can be important in both diagnosing their problem and helping them overcome.

The Word of God:

Proverbs 11:25

"The generous man will be prosperous, and he who waters will himself be watered."

Proverbs 21:26

"All day long he is craving, while the righteous gives and does not hold back."

Proverbs 28:27

"He who gives to the poor will never want, but he who shuts his eyes will have many curses."

Matthew 10:8

"...Freely you received, freely give."

Matthew 10:42

"And whoever in the name of disciple gives to one of these little ones even a cup of cold water to drink, truly I say to you, he shall not lose his reward."

2 Corinthians 9:7

"Let each one do just as he has purposed in his heart; not grudgingly or under compulsion; for God loves a cheerful giver."

GLUTTONY

Definition:

A glutton is a person who eats and drinks excessively or voraciously. It can also speak of a person who has a remarkable desire or capacity for something, like a glutton for work.

Brief Explanation:

Gluttony is not the same as a weight problem. Being overweight is a problem, a health problem especially in Western culture. But Gluttony is different. It is out of control eating or drinking, usually driven by greed, lust or deep emotional "hunger." A glutton is out of control, and the issue again is not weight, but gaining control of the desire to continue to eat for secondary gain, or to meet a need that cannot be met. Finding the need, developing a strategy to meet the need in legitimate ways is the key, using sensitivity and care.

The Word of God:

Proverbs 23:1

"When you sit down to dine with a ruler, consider carefully what is before you; and put a knife to your throat, If you are man of great appetite."

Proverbs 23:21

"For the heavy drinker and the glutton will come to poverty, and drowsiness will clothe a man with rags."

Matthew 11:19

"The Son of Man came eating and drinking, and they say behold a gluttonous man and a drunkard, a friend of tax-gathers and sinners! Yet wisdom is vindicated by her deeds."

1Corinthians 10:7

"And do not be idolaters, as some of them were, as it is written, "The people sat down to eat and drink, and stood up to play."

1 Corinthians 10:31

"Whether, then, you eat or drink or whatever you do, do all to the glory of God."

GOALS

Definition:

The purpose toward which an endeavor is directed; an objective.

Brief Explanation:

In counseling, it is helpful to establish goals for the purpose for the counseling process. I often ask a counselee, how long do you think the counseling will take and what do you expect to get from it. Some respond realistically, some not, generally a reflection of their way of seeing the world. Some have expectations that are realistic (to help me cope, to learn more, to grow up) some are not (to completely alter my personality, to make everyone like me, to find a husband/wife, etc.). Setting or establishing goals that are definable, measurable and obtainable within a reasonable time frame is an effective counseling strategy.

The Word of God:
Psalm 37:4, 5

"Delight yourself in the Lord; and He will give you the desires of your heart. Commit your way to the Lord, trust also in Him, and He will do it."

1 Corinthians 9:24, 25

"Do you not know that those who run in a race all run, but only one receives the prize? Run in such a way that you may win. Everyone who competes in the games exercises self-control in all things. They then do it to receive a perishable wreath, but we an imperishable."

Galatians 6:9

"Let us not lose heart in doing good, for in due time we will reap if we do not grow weary."

GRIEF

Definition:

Grief is a deep mental anguish, as that arising from bereavement. It is a source of deep mental anguish, due to loss, whether by death, situation, or other relationship.

Brief Explanation:

Grief is a process, beginning with a traumatic (to the client) event in their life. Issues of death and dying will frequently be encountered in counseling. Being aware of the common reactions people may have during the dying process and for the bereaved after the loss of a loved one, is essential to good counsel and care in general.

As covered under the topic of death above, grieving is often misunderstood. It is thoroughly biblical and healthy to grieve, mourn but if believers, not without hope. That is, we grieve our loss (blessed are those who mourn, for they shall be comforted) but with the knowledge that to be absent in the body is to be present in the Lord. Glib "he or she is in a better place" or "God needed your mom or dad more than you" can be cruel, and are to be avoided. The ministry of presence, listening, empathetically, is the best medicine for one in times of grief. Of course, watch for delayed responses, sometimes years later of unresolved grief. See *Grief Relief* by Dr Stan DeKoven.

The Word of God:

Matthew 5:4

Blessed are those who mourn, for they shall be comforted.

John 11:35, 36

Jesus wept. So the Jews were saying, "See how He loved him!"

John 14:1

"Believe Me that I am in the Father and the Father is in Me; otherwise believe because of the works themselves."

1 Peter 1:3-5

"Blessed be the God and Father of our Lord Jesus Christ, who according to His great mercy has caused us to be born again to a living hope through the resurrection of Jesus Christ from the dead, to obtain an inheritance which is imperishable and undefiled and will not fade away, reserved in heaven for you, who are protected by the power of God through faith for a salvation ready to be revealed in the last time."

1 Thessalonians 4:13, 14

"But we do not want you to be uninformed, brethren, about those who are asleep, so that you will not grieve as do the rest who have no hope. For if we believe that Jesus died and rose again, even so God will bring with Him those who have fallen asleep in Jesus."

GUILT

Definition:

Guilt is the fact of being responsible for the commission of an offense.

This guilt can be due to culpability for a crime or lesser breach of regulations that carries a legal penalty. Further, it is a remorseful awareness of having done something wrong, and with it self-reproach for supposed inadequacy or wrongdoing.

Brief Explanation:

Guilt is different than shame, which is covered in some detail below. Guilt usually is a feeling, or a conscious awareness that ones attitude or behavior has violated some agreed upon rule of life. It is the experience of feeling remorseful, genuinely sorry for having done something to hurt someone else or breaking a given code. Guilt is healthy if there is indeed something that has been done wrong by the person, and the answer for it is confession, repentance, and if necessary restitution. However, the problem often seen in counseling is in working with someone with too much guilt (overwhelming guilt over minor things, or things they in fact did not do or were not responsible for, such as the victim of abuse) or too little guilt (for a sociopath, such as a criminal or drug addict with no sense of responsibility for ones behavior). In either case, reality is what is needed, or an honest appraisal, in light of the word of God, of the behavior of the individual. It is important not to maximize or minimize guilt, but lead the client to resolution of it beginning with an honest appraisal or diagnosis of the guilty offense, and a biblical response, as noted above.

The Word of God:

Psalm 32:3, 5

"When I kept silent about my sin, my body wasted away through my groaning all day long. I acknowledged my sin to You, and my iniquity I did not hide; I said, "I will confess my transgressions to the Lord"; And You forgave the guilt of my sin."

Psalm 103:12

"As far as the east if from the west, so far has He removed our transgressions from us."

2 Chronicles 30:9

"For the Lord your God is gracious and compassionate, and will not turn His face away from you if you return to Him."

HEALING

Definition:

Healing means to restore to health or soundness; cure. It is also defined as to set right; repair: *healed the rift between us.* Another view is to restore (a person) to spiritual wholeness.

Brief Explanation:

In I Corinthians 12: 9, Paul states that there are "gifts of healing", plural. Thus, there are many ways the Lord heals, all of which are to be active in the Body of Christ. Counseling is called the talking cure, in that, it is believed that through talking out a problem, relief, solutions, healing of the problem can come. This is often true, but of course, the talk must be in light of biblical solutions and common sense. As Christian Counselors, to believe the Lord with a client for healing, to pray for such, to expect the Lord to heal through a variety of means is appropriate. However we must remember that character does not need healing, but maturation, and many conditions, such as depression, anxiety, and certainly thought disorders take time, and often a multidisciplinary approach, that is, medicine, counseling and prayer.

The Word of God:

James 5:13-16

"Is anyone among you suffering? Then he must pray. Is anyone cheerful? He is to sing praises. Is anyone among you sick? The he must call for the elders of the church and they are to pray over him, anointing him with oil in the name of the Lord; and the prayer offered in faith will restore the one who is sick, and the Lord will raise him up, and if he has committed sins, they will be forgiven him. Therefore, confess your sins to one another, and pray for one another so that you may be healed. The effective prayer of a righteous man can accomplish much."

Isaiah 40:29, 31

"He gives strength to the weary, and to him who lacks might he increases power. Yet those who wait for the Lord will gain new strength; they will mount up with wings like eagles, they will run and not get tired, they will walk and not become weary."

Jeremiah 30:17

"For I will restore you to health and I will heal you of your wounds, declares the Lord, Because they have called you an outcast, saying: it is Zion; no one cares for her."

Psalm 103:1

"Bless the Lord, O my soul, And all that is within me, bless His holy name. Who pardons all your iniquities, who heals all your diseases."

Psalm 147:3

"He heals the broken hearted and bind up their wounds."

1 Peter 2:24

"And He himself bore our sins in His body on the cross, so that we might die to sin and live to righteousness; for by His wounds we are healed."

HEAVEN

Definition:

Heaven is defined differently by different people, but generally can be defined as the sky or universe as seen from the earth; the firmament. Often used in the plural. Within Christianity, Heaven is the abode of God, the angels, and the souls of those who are granted salvation. It is an eternal state of communion with God; everlasting bliss.

Brief Explanation: It has been said, everyone wants to go to Heaven, but no body wants to die. However, heaven is, for the believer, a real hope, and something to look forward to. Often, heaven and hell are topics that are discussed in light of the loss of a loved one, or in working with a dying patient. There is nothing more important than to give comfort to the bereaved, and where possible, give hope to the client of a heaven to gain. If the client you are working with is unsure of their destination when they die, and they are open to discuss spiritual things, it is a wonderful opportunity to introduce the joy of knowing Christ to them. Again, sensitivity is needed in discussing eternal things, and we we should do so with humility and grace.

The Word of God:

Genesis 1:1

"In the beginning, God created the heavens and the earth."

Matthew 6:9

"Pray then in this way, Our Father, who art in Heaven,

Hallowed be Thy name."

John 14:2

"In my Father's house are many dwelling places; if it were not so, I would have told you; for I go to prepare a place for you."

Acts 1:11

"Men of Galilee, why do you stand looking into the sky? This Jesus, who has been taken up from you into heaven, will come in just the same way as you have watched Him go into heaven."

1 Corinthians 15:51, 52

"Behold, I tell you a mystery; we will not all sleep, but we will all be changed, in a moment, in the twinkling of an eye, at the last trumpet; for the trumpet will sound, and the dead will be raised imperishable, and we will be changed."

Philippians 3: 20

"For our citizenship is in heaven, from which also we eagerly wait for our Savior, the Lord Jesus Christ."

1 John 3:2

"And He Himself is the propitiation for our sins; and not for ours only, but also for those of the whole world."

HOME

Definition:

Home is a place where one lives; a residence, which includes the physical structure within which one lives, such as a house or apartment. Further, it is a dwelling place together with the family or social unit that occupies it; a household. This is an environment offering security and happiness; a valued place regarded as a refuge or place of origin. Also, it is the place, such as a country or town, where one was born or has lived for a long period, our native habitat, as of a plant or animal. It is the place where something is discovered, founded, developed, or promoted; a source.

Brief Explanation:

Ah, hearth and home; a man's castle and a woman's security. Sadly, especially seen in pastoral or Christian counseling, this is often not the case. A happy home is not a myth in Western Nations, but it is certainly under siege. What constitutes a happy or health home? What environment must be created to have a happy or healthy home? What skills are needed to have a happy marriage, family, children, etc.? These are the kinds of questions that Christian counselors need to be ready to address, as they are commonly discussed in counseling. It is best to be armed with scripture and wisdom from professionals who are balanced in their biblical and psychological view, and tread carefully in the home of your client. For more, see Dr. DeKoven's books *Marriage and Family Life* and *Parenting on Purpose*.

The Word of God:

Joshua 24:15

"....Choose for yourselves today whom you will serve; but as for me and my house, we will serve the Lord."

Mark 5:19

"....go home to your people and report to them what great things the Lord has done for you, and how he had mercy on you."

Matthew 12:48-50

"But he answered the one who was telling him and said, "Who is my mother and who are my brothers? And stretching out his hand toward his disciples, he said, behold my mother and my brothers! For whoever shall do he will of my Father who is in heaven, he is my brother and sister and mother."

John 19:27

"The he said to the disciple, Behold your mother! And from that hour the disciple took her into his own household."

I Timothy 5:4

"But if any widow has children or grandchildren, let them first learn to practice piety in regard to their own family, and to make some return to their parents; for this is acceptable in the sight of God. "

Psalms 127:1

"Except the Lord build the house they labor in vain who build it."

Ephesians 6:1-4

"Children obey your parents in the Lord, for this is right. Honor you Father and Mother (which is the first commandment with a promise) that it may be well with you and that you may live long in the earth. And fathers, do not provoke your children to anger; but bring them up in the discipline and instruction of the Lord."

HOMOSEXUALITY

Definition:

A complex combination of attraction and behavior, where by a person is attracted to the same sex, and acts out sexually towards a member of the same sex.

Brief Explanation:

Homosexuality is a complex and controversial issue in modern culture. Debate has roared as to how the church should view and act towards a person with same sex attraction and action. Some of the debate deals with the origin or cause of homosexuality (nature; I was born that way vs. nurture, I became this way or chose to be this way). As of this writing, there is no definitive evidence that a person is born with a same sex attraction; however, it would also be naive to believe that a young person woke up one day and declared "I want to be gay!!!"

Our best view of this psychological and spiritual problem is that some (latest statistics seem to confirm 2-3% of the population are homosexual, not 10% as gay activists purport) men and women (but mainly men) are born with a predisposition towards effeminate behavior, and there are developmental, family and social dynamics that add to the potential of a person becoming homosexual.

Biblically, homosexual behavior is condemned, as is effeminate behavior. To be tempted or to have an orientation towards the same sex is not the same as sin. God's intention, from the beginning, has been one woman, one man, one lifetime; Adam and Eve, not Adam and Steve.

So, what if someone is in homosexual sin, and wants to change...is change possible? Well, the short answer is yes...the long answer is it takes much time, hard work, and one must have a realistic goal, which is first celibacy and singleness, contentment with the Lord, and perhaps as healing occurs, a heterosexual relationship. For someone struggling with homosexuality, but who has not acted out, truth in love is needed. Men and women struggling with homosexuality need support, accountability, healing and love...like every person in the body of Christ.

For more on this topic, see Joe Dallas' dynamic book *Desires in Conflict*.

The Word of God:

Genesis 1:26,27

"Then God said, Let us make man in Our image, according to our likeness...and God made man in His own image, in the image of God he created him; male and female he created them."

Leviticus 18:22

"You shall not lie with a male as one lies with a female; it is an abomination."

Romans 1:26-27

"For this reason God gave them over to degrading passions; for heir women exchanged the natural function for that which is unnatural, and in the same way also the men abandoned the natural function of the woman and burned in their desire towards one another, men with men committing indecent acts and receiving in their own persons the due penalty of their error."

1 Corinthians 6:9, 11

"Or do you not know that the unrighteous shall not inherit the kingdom of God? Do not be deceived; neither fornicators, nor idolaters, nor adulterers, nor effeminate, nor homosexuals. And such were some of you; but you were washed, but you were sanctified, but you were justified in the mane of the Lord Jesus Christ, and in the Spirit of our God."

HONESTY

Definition:

Honesty is the quality or condition of being honest; integrity. A component of honesty, truthfulness or sincerity.

Brief Explanation:

In Billy Joel's song *Honesty,* he states it is a word hardly heard, and desperately needed. Sad but often true, even in Christian circles. I have heard told more than once men and women who have gone to "Christian Mechanics or Realtors", only to report how disappointed they were, due to dishonest business practices. Similar things are stated about spiritual leaders who say one thing and do another; whom the bible calls hypocrites.

Honesty does not, on the other hand, mean brutality. If fact, speaking the truth in love is to be a quality found in every believer. Honesty, it may be hardly heard, but should be a seen in the lives, business dealings and spiritual ministry of God's people.

The Word of God:

Luke 8:11, 15

"Now the parable is this: the seed is the word of God. But the seed in the good soil, these are the ones who have heard the word in an honest and good heart, and hold it fast, and bear fruit with perseverance."

Psalm 24:3, 4

"Indeed, none of those who wait for you will be ashamed; those who deal treacherously without cause will be ashamed. Make me know Your ways, O Lord; teach me Your paths."

Proverbs 16:8

"Better is a little with righteousness than great income with injustice."

Romans 12:17

"Never pay back evil for evil to anyone. Respect what is right in the sight of all men."

2 Corinthians 13:7

"Now we pray to God that you do no wrong; not that we ourselves may appear approved, but that you may do what is right, even though we should appear unapproved."

HOPE

Definition:

Hope is the feeling that what is wanted can be had or that event will turn out well. It can include looking forward to something with desire and reasonable confidence, to believe, desire or trust.

Brief Explanation:

Many people come to counseling with an ever increasing and overwhelming sense of hopelessness. Hope is a key component for healing, but is not always easy to find in the midst of what seems hopeless.

Counselors can help by coming along side of a client and, as it were, lending your faith and hope to the client. Just knowing that you are a caring person, and are willing to walk with a person in a time of need provides enough hope that with God's help normalcy in life will return. Of course, we do not want to give false hope (guarantee of healing, health, prosperity, etc.), but real hope in God and the healing process he has provided to his children.

The Word of God:

1 Corinthians 13:7, 13

"Bears all things, believes all things, hopes all things, endures all things. But now abides faith, hope, love, these three; and the greatest of these is love."

Colossians1:27

"To whom God was pleased to make known what is the riches of the glory of this mystery among the Gentiles, which is Christ in you, the hope in glory"

Titus 3:7

"...that, being justified by his grace, we might be made heirs according to the hope of eternal life."

Hebrews 6:19

"...which we have as an anchor of the soul, a hope both sure and steadfast and entering into that which is within the veil;"

Hebrews 11:1

"Now faith is assurance of things hoped for, a conviction of things not seen."

1 Peter 1:3

"Blessed be the God and Father of our Lord Jesus Christ, who according to his great mercy begat us again unto a living hope by the resurrection of Jesus Christ from the dead,"

HUMILITY

Definition:

The quality or condition of being humble.

Brief Explanation:

A humble person is not merely self-effacing. He or she is a person with an honest appraisal of themselves in terms of their strengths and weaknesses. They have learned to accept themselves as they are, without accepting sin or a weakness that may be overcome. Jesus was the meekest of all, having a quiet strength of character; he was also humble, in that he rightly knew who he was, and who he wasn't, and what he was called to do. A humble person is one who can be admired. Being humble, a Christian counselor never oversells or undersells his or her skills, and always acknowledges that it is by the grace of God and the skills learned that we are able to do what we do. As Paul stated so aptly, it is in him we live and move and have our very existence; we should always be grateful.

The Word of God:

Philippians 2:5-8

"Have this attitude in yourselves which was also in Christ Jesus, who, although He existed in the form of God, did not regard equality with God a thing to be grasped, but emptied Himself, taking the form of a bond-servant, and being made in the likeness of men. Being found in appearance as a man, He humbled Himself by becoming obedient to the point of death on the cross."

2 Chronicles 7:14

"And My people who are called by My name humble themselves and pray and seek My face and turn from their wicked ways, then I will hear from heaven, will forgive their sin and will heal their land."

Proverbs 15:33

"The fear of the Lord is instruction for wisdom, and before honor comes humility."

Matthew 18:4

"Whoever then humbles himself as this child, he is the greatest in the kingdom of heaven."

James 4:6

"God is opposed to the proud, but gives grace to the humble."

1 Peter 5:6

"Therefore humble yourselves under the mighty hand of God, that He may exalt you at the proper time."

INCEST

Definition:

Incest is defined as sexual relations between persons who are so closely related that their marriage is illegal or forbidden by custom. It is also the statutory crime of sexual relations with a near relative.

Brief Explanation:

Probably one of the most difficult situations to have to counsel is that of incest or child sexual abuse in the home. Generally, incest is seen differently than pedophilia, as the inappropriate and damaging sexual abuse occurs in isolation of the family. Of course, in either case, the perpetrator if known must be reported to the Child Welfare or Police in your community.

Incest is forbidden in all civilized cultures, is forbidden in the bible, and is to be dealt with directly and seriously. Often, the perpetrator will end up in jail for a season, often, but not always, causing the break up of the family. To handle a case of incest takes skill and sensitivity, and often specialized training. For more, see *Family Violence: Patterns of Destruction* by Dr. Stan DeKoven

The Word of God:
Leviticus 18:6, 7

"None of you shall approach any blood relative of his to uncover nakedness; I am the Lord. You shall not uncover the nakedness of your father, that is, the nakedness of your mother. She is your mother; you are not to uncover her nakedness."

Leviticus 18:29

"For whoever does any of these abominations, those persons who do so shall be cut off from among their people."

Leviticus 20:12

"If there is a man who lies with his daughter-in-law, both of them shall surely be put to death; they have committed incest, their blood guiltiness is upon them."

Psalm 27:10

"For my father and my mother have forsaken me, but the Lord will take my up."

Isaiah 41:10, 11, 13

"Do not fear, for I am with you; do not anxiously look about you, for I am your God. I will strengthen you, surely I will help you, surely I will uphold you with My righteous right hand. Behold, all those who are angered at you will be shamed and dishonored; those who contend with you will be as nothing and will perish. For I am the Lord your God, who upholds your right hand, who says to you, do not fear, I will help you."

LONELINESS

Definition:

Loneliness is to be without companions; alone. It is characterized by loneliness or being solitary. It is being unfrequented by people; it can also mean desolate: *a lonely crossroads* or dejected by the awareness of being alone.

Brief Explanation:

Loneliness is endemic in Western culture. Men are looking for women, women for men. Even in the midst of a church, lonely people commiserate their loneliness.

Being lonely is not always a matter of how many people you relate to. It is often a state of mind, of feeling unloved and insignificant in the midst of people. This is by far the deeper issue, the one often addressed in counseling. Most lonely people feel unwanted for some reason, and must learn to accept themselves and God's appraisal of them. Dr. Chant in his outstanding book *Dazzling Secrets for Despondent Saints* addresses this condition, urging men of faith to first find their significance in God. We are a New Creation in Christ, loved by God, significant in him, and important in God's economy. Accepting this, putting on Jesus Christ makes a major difference in the sense of worthiness of individuals. Once one feels worthy of care, becoming friendly and engaged follows, and loneliness lessens for most. Loneliness is a real problem; the solution for most is Christ and his church.

The Word of God:
Psalm 68:5

"A father of the fatherless and a judge for the widows, Is God in His holy habitation."

Psalm 46:1-3

"God is our refuge and strength, A very present help in trouble. Therefore we will not fear, though the earth should change And though the mountains slip into the heart of the sea; Though its water roar and foam, Though the mountains quake at its swelling pride."

Proverbs 18:24

"A man of many friends comes to ruin, But there is a friend who sticks closer than a brother."

Genesis 28:15

"Behold, I am with you and will keep you wherever you go, and will bring you back to this land; for I will not leave you until I have done what I have promised you."

John 14:18

"I will not leave you as orphans; I will come to you."

Hebrews 13:5,6

"Make sure that your character is free from the love of money, being content with what you have; for He Himself has said, "I will never desert you, nor will I ever forsake you," so that we confidently say, "The Lord is my helper, I will not be afraid. What will man do to me?"

Matthew 28:20

"...teaching them to observe all that I commanded you; and lo, I am with you always, even to the end of the age."

LOVE

Definition:

A deep, tender, ineffable feeling of affection and solicitude toward a person, such as that arising from kinship, recognition of attractive qualities, or a sense of underlying oneness defines love. It can also be defined as a feeling of intense desire and attraction toward a person with whom one is disposed to make a pair; the emotion of sex and romance.

Brief Explanation: There are four words used for love in the ancient Greek language. They are Eros, Storge, Philea and Agape. Each signifies a different type or quality of love. The first speaks of romantic or sexual love, the second of family love or devotion, the third to friendships or brotherly love, and the last to the unselfish or altruistic love exhibited by God himself. All forms of love stated here are valid in their respective places. We all need love. Carl Rogers called love in the counseling situation unconditional positive regard. This means, we accept the person as they are, warts and all, without judgment. From a Christian viewpoint, we accept the sinner, but not the sin. The demonstration of love, especially for the wounded soul who has been raised in a love impoverished environment, is one of the gifts a counselor or pastor can bring to the counseling relationship. It must be demonstrated appropriately, for the benefit of the other, but establishing an environment of empathy, warmth, respect and trust between the client and the counselor. (For more on the Four Loves, see Dr. Ken Chant's *Christian Life: Patterns of Gracious Living*).

The Word of God:
1 John 4:10

"In this is love, not that we loved God, but that He loved us and sent His Son to be the propitiation for our sins."

John 3:16

"For God so loved the world, that He gave His only begotten Son, that whoever believes in Him shall not perish, but have eternal life."

1 John 3:1

"See how great a love the Father has bestowed on us, that we would be called children of God; and such we are. For this reason the world does not know us, because it did not know Him."

Romans 12:9,10

"Let love be without hypocrisy. Abhor what is evil; cling to what is good. Be devoted to one another in brotherly love; give preference to one another in honor;"

John 13:34,35

"A new commandment I give to you, that you love one another, even as I have loved you, that you also love one another. By this all men will know that you are My disciples, if you have love for one another."

1 Corinthians 13:4-8

"Love is patient, love is kind and is not jealous; love does not brag and is not arrogant, does not act unbecomingly; it does not seek its own, is not provoked, does not take into account a wrong suffered, does not rejoice in unrighteousness, but rejoices with the truth; bears all things, believes all things, hopes all things, endures all things. Love never fails; but if there are gifts of prophecy, they will be done away; if there are tongues, they will cease; if there is knowledge, it will be done away."

LUST

Definition:

Lust is defined as deep desire, especially an intense sexual desire or appetite, often uncontrolled. It can also speak of an ardent enthusiasm or zest for life, yearning or desire, strong craving.

Brief Explanation:

It has been said that hate is the opposite of love; but in many ways, lust is. That is, lust is to desire something good, made by God, in an illegitimate way. To lust is to so deeply desire or want something, especially of a sexual nature, that it overwhelms the normal senses of right and wrong.

From a Christian viewpoint, we accept the sinner as they are, but not the sin. The proper response to lust, as former President Jimmy Carter said "in my heart" is repentance, and to turn to God for his love and the love of others in appropriate expression. Many men and women suffer deeply due to the lust of the flesh, lust of the eyes, and are in need of deep healing that begins with understanding Gods' ways of healing and restoration found in His word. Again, one of the gifts a counselor or pastor can bring to the counseling relationship is true love demonstrated appropriately, for the benefit of the other, by establishing an environment of empathy, warmth, respect and trust between the client and the counselor.

(For more on the Four Loves, see Dr. Ken Chant's *Christian Life: Patterns of Gracious Living*).

The Word of God:
Proverbs 6:25

"Lust not after her beauty in thy heart; Neither let her take thee with her eyelids."

Matthew 5:28

"But I say unto you, that every one that looks on a woman to lust after her hath committed adultery with her already in his heart."

Romans 1:27

"And likewise also the men, leaving the natural use of the woman, burned in their lust one toward another, men with men working unseemliness, and receiving in themselves that recompense of their error which was due."

1Corinthians 10:6

"Now these things were our examples, to the intent we should not lust after evil things, as they also lusted."

Galatians 5:16, 17

"But I say, walk by the Spirit, and ye shall not fulfill the lust of the flesh. For the flesh lusts against the Spirit, and the Spirit against the flesh; for these are contrary the one to the other; that ye may not do things that ye would."

Ephesians 2:3

"Among whom we also all once lived in the lust of our flesh, doing the desires of the flesh and of the mind, and were by nature children of wrath, even as the rest."

James 1:14, 15

"But each man is tempted, when he is drawn away by his own lust, and enticed. Then the lust, when it hath conceived, bears sin: and the sin, when it is full grown, brings forth death."

1Peter 2:11

"Beloved, I beseech you as sojourners and pilgrims, to abstain from fleshly lust, which war against the soul;"

1Peter 2:10

"But chiefly them that walk after the flesh in the lust of defilement, and despise dominion. Daring, self-willed, they tremble not to rail at dignities:

1John 2:16, 17

"For all that is in the world, the lust of the flesh and the lust of the eyes and the vain glory of life, is not of the Father, but is of the world. And the world passes away, and the lust thereof: but he that doeth the will of God abides for ever."

MARRIAGE

Definition:

Marriage is defined as the legal union of a man and woman as husband and wife. It is the state of being married; wedlock.

Brief Explanation:

Second in importance to our relationship with Christ and his church is the covenant of marriage. Marriage is not merely a legal agreement between two people (Adam and Eve), but is a covenant, a binding agreement that from the beginning was never to be broken. To have a successful marriage requires several things, to include maturity, love, sacrifice, discipline, compatibility, etc. From a biblical view, maturity and common faith are all that is required, but this does not disallow common sense in choosing a mate for life. Paul described two overriding characteristics of a healthy marriage, which are the blending of Love and Respect.

Matches are not made in heaven but on earth, by well intentioned but often flawed people. Though marriage is to be till death do us part, not all will make it (approximately 50% of first marriages end in divorce, and 70% of second marriages), yet we must hold the sacred and sanctity of marriage high and not lower the standards of scripture. Where failure occurs, grace, mercy forgiveness and restoration are needed and readily available. For more see Dr. Stan DeKoven's *Marriage and Family Life: A Christian Perspective* and Dr. Ken Chant's *To the Corinthians*

The Word of God:

Genesis 2:18, 23, 24

"Then the Lord God said, "It is not good for the man to be alone; I will make him a helper suitable for him." The man said, "This is now bone of my bones, And flesh of my flesh; She shall be called woman, because she was taken out of Man." For this reason a man shall leave his father and his mother, and be joined to his wife; and they shall become one flesh."

Proverbs 18:22

"He who finds a wife finds a good thing And obtains favor from the Lord."

2 Corinthians 6:14

"Do not be bound together with unbelievers; for what partnership have righteousness and lawlessness, or what fellowship has light with darkness?"

Ephesians 5:21,22

"...and be subject to one another in the fear of Christ. Wives, be subject to your own husbands, as to the Lord."

1 Peter 3:7

"You husbands in the same way, live with your wives in an understanding way, as with someone weaker, since she is a woman; and show her honor as a fellow heir of the grace of life, so that your prayers will not be hindered."

Ephesians 5:25

"Husbands, love our wives, just as Christ also loved the church and gave Himself up for her,"

Ephesians 5:33

"Nevertheless, each individual among you also is to love his own wife even as himself, and the wife must see to it that she respects her husband."

Hebrews 13:4

"Marriage is to be held in honor among all, and the marriage bed is to be undefiled; for fornicators and adulterers God will judge."

1 Corinthians 7:4-7

"The wife does not have authority over her own body, but the husband does; and likewise also the husband does not have authority over his own body, but the wife does. Stop depriving one another, except by agreement for a time, so that you may devote yourselves to prayer, and come together again so that Satan will not tempt you because of your lack of self-control. But this I say by way of concession, not of command. Yet I wish that all men were even as I myself am. However, each man has his own gift from God, one in this manner, and another in that."

Ecclesiastes 9:9

"Enjoy life with the woman whom you love all the days of your fleeting life which He has given to you under the sun; for this is your reward in life and in your toil in which you have labored under the sun."

MIRACLES

Definition:

An event that appears inexplicable by the laws of nature and so is held to be supernatural in origin or an act of God

Brief Explanation:

The phrase "It's a Miracle" is thrown around in common discussion for the most trivial things (such us that a husband came home on time). Truthfully, miracles of healing are rare and incredible; that is why they are called a miracle. I believe in miracles. I have seen and experienced miraculous healings in people; they defy logic, but God still does them, according to his sovereignty. As counselors, there will be clients you work with that seems beyond hope, and when they experience healing, restoration, or overcome a life debilitating problem, it seems miraculous, and maybe it is, if it defies logic, is beyond natural ability, and fits into the sovereign purpose of God. Believe in miracles; trust God for the supernatural; God may just surprise you.

The Word of God:

Exodus 34:10

"Then God said, "Behold, I am going to make a covenant. Before all your people I will perform miracles which have not been produced in all the earth, nor among any of the nations; and all the people among whom you live will see the working of the Lord, for it is a fearful thing that I am going to perform with you."

Psalm 77:14

"You are the God who works wonders; you have made known your strength among the peoples."

Acts 4:22

"For the man was more than forty years old on whom this miracle of healing had been performed."

Acts 8:13

"And Simon also believed; and being baptized, he continued with Philip; and saw many signs and great miracles; he was amazed."

1Corinthians 12:28

"And God has placed some in the church, first apostles, secondly prophets, thirdly teachers, and then miracles, then gifts of healings, helps, governments, and different kinds of tongues."

MONEY

Definition:

Money is a medium that can be exchanged for goods and services and is used as a measure of their values on the market, including among its forms a commodity such as gold, an officially issued coin or note, or a deposit in a checking account or other readily liquefiable account.

Brief Explanation:

In Western culture, it is rarely the lack of money that is the pervasive problem, but the poor stewardship of the money God provides is the problem. The usage of money often defines the priorities of a person's life and where a person spends his or her money defines the condition of the heart. Thus, money is an issue. It often comes up in counseling, as people are looking for a "bargain price" for the help they need. The laborer is worth of hire, and if you have put several years of time and energy, let alone your money into preparing to help people in counseling, you should expect to be paid for your services. Free is just what it is worth; nothing. So do put a value on your time and expertise, and be aware of how a person spends and manages money...it is often a window to the soul you are trying to help. (For more on this topic, see DeKoven and Wyns, *Living Fruitfully*, and Dick Edic's *Resourcing the Vision: Comprehensive Guide to Stewardship*)

The Word of God:
Ecclesiastes 5:10

"He who loves money will not be satisfied with money, nor he who loves abundance with its income. This too is vanity."

Ecclesiastes 10:19

"Men prepare a meal for enjoyment, and wine makes life merry, and money is the answer to everything."

1 Timothy 6:10

"For the love of money is a root of all sorts of evil, and some by longing for it have wandered away from the faith and pierced themselves with many grief's."

Psalm 37:16

"Better is the little of the righteous than the abundance of many wicked."

Luke 16:10,11

"He who is faithful in a very little thing is faithful also in much; and he who is unrighteous in a very little thing is unrighteous also in much. Therefore is you have not been faithful in the use of unrighteous wealth, who will entrust the true riches to you?"

Philippians 4:19

"And my God will supply all your needs according to His riches in glory in Christ Jesus."

OBEDIENCE

Definition:

Obedience is the quality or condition of being obedient; the act of obeying.

Brief Explanation:

When my children were young, in the last century, I used to tell them "remember, to obey is better than being sacrificed!" Well, it worked for a while. Of course, children are to learn to obey their parents; wives are to show respect, but obedience is not required. We are to serve our employers according to the contract we work under and have agreed to, and we are to absolutely obey God and his word. It is in the first and last area where obedience is needed and is often problematic for people.

Many people come for counseling due to disobedience to God's laws, or not understanding what God expects. For example, a man came for counseling due to his confusion over his choices in relationships. He was married, for over 20 years, but had a girlfriend that made him happier. His statement was, "doesn't God want me to be happy?" My response surprised him when I emphatically stated "no!" "God is more interested in your holiness than your happiness."

To obey is to follow what is right, based upon the rightness of the person making the demand. Parents do not have to be right all the time, but it is their right to expect their children to be obedient (up to age 12 or so, then they are to learn to honor their parents). God is always right; those who love him keep his commandments; even when it is difficult. Counselors, though empathic with the situations of people, must continue to hold to biblical standards.

The Word of God:

Deuteronomy 11:26-28

"See, I am setting before you today a blessing and a curse: the blessing, if you listen to the commandments of the Lord you God, which I am commanding you today; and the curse, if you do not listen to the commandments of the Lord your God, but turn aside from the way which I am commanding you today, by following other gods which you have not known."

Deuteronomy 27:10

"You shall write on the stones all the words of this law very distinctly."

John 14:15,23

"If you love Me, you will keep My commandments." Jesus answered and said to him, "If anyone loves Me, he will keep My word; and My Father will love him, and We will come to him and make Our abode with him."

1 John 5:3

"For this is the love of God, that we keep His commandments; and His commandments are not burdensome."

PARENTS

Definition:

A parent is one who begets, gives birth to, or nurtures and raises a child; a father or mother. A parent can include any ancestor; a progenitor. It can also include a guardian; a protector.

Brief Explanation:

Parenting is a difficult task, especially in the fast paced change a minute world we live in. Parents must be more determined than ever to guard and guide their children.

Many parents approach the task with planning, many without a clue. Often, when problems arise in the children, the parents are desperate for answers. Since each situation is different, the best advice is often to present principles, and then see what has worked in the past and try some new things to help the situation.

Parenting should be purposeful, developmentally sensitive, biblical in terms of principle, and flexible, since blessed are the flexible, they shall not be broken. For more, see *Parenting on Purpose* by Dr. Stan DeKoven.

The Word of God:

Leviticus 19:3

"Every one of you shall reverence his mother and his father, and you shall keep My Sabbaths; I am the Lord your God."

Proverbs 22:6

"Train up a child in the way he should go, even when he is old he will not depart from it."

Proverbs 23:13

"Do not hold back discipline from the child."

Ephesians 6:1-3

"Children, obey your parents in the Lord, for this is right. Honor your father and mother (which is the first commandment with a promise), so that it may be well with you, and that you may live long on the earth."

PATIENCE

Definition:

Patience is the capacity, quality, or fact of being patient. Patience emphasizes calmness, self-control, and the willingness or ability to tolerate delay or to delay gratification.

Brief Explanation:

"Dear Lord, give me patience, and give it to me now!" Not the brightest of prayers, but understandable. Patience, especially with ones self or family member is a necessary ingredient to the healing process for most. It takes time to create a problem, and it takes time to see the problem resolved.

Counselors need patience as well. The process of change is a time consuming one, and is in the hands of the Lord and the person being helped. Patience, the ability to give time a chance is a great virtue, and one we as counselors need to practice.

The Word of God:

Psalm 37:7

"Rest in the Lord and wait patiently for Him; Do not fret because of him who prospers in his way, Because of the man who carries out wicked schemes."

Hebrews 10:36

"For you have need of endurance, so that when you have done the will of God, you may receive what was promised."

Galatians 5:22

"But the fruit of the Spirit is…patience…"

James 1:4

"And let endurance have its perfect result, so that you may be perfect and complete, lacking in nothing."

PEACE

Definition:

Peace is the absence of war or other hostilities. Further, it is an agreement or a treaty to end hostilities. It can also be seen as freedom from quarrels and disagreement; harmonious relations, such as roommates living in peace with each other. Finally, peace is inner contentment; serenity: *peace of mind.*

Brief Explanation:

Many clients coming for counseling are stressed and anxious…they lack peace. This can be caused by physical stress, emotional upheaval due to relational difficulties, wrong choices and sin. Helping the client find peace means to assist them to resolve problems that are causing the lack of peace. This can include changes in habits, stress reduction, resolving conflicts in relationships including with God, etc. Helping someone find peace in life is helping them experience the Kingdom of God as the Lord promised.

The Word of God:

John 14:27

"Peace I leave with you; My peace I give to you; not as the world gives do I give to you. Do not let your heart be troubled, nor let it be fearful."

Romans 5:1

"Therefore, having been justified by faith, we have peace with God through our Lord Jesus Christ..."

Colossians 1:20

"...and through Him to reconcile all things to Himself, having made peace through the blood of His cross; through Him, I say, whether things on earth or things in heaven."

Philippians 4:7

"And the peace of God, which surpasses all comprehension, will guard your hearts and your minds in Christ Jesus."

Galatians 5:22

"But the fruit of the Spirit is...peace..."

John 16:33

"These things I have spoken to you, so that in Me you may have peace. In the world you have tribulation, but take courage; I have overcome the world."

James 1:4

"And let endurance have its perfect result, so that you may be perfect and complete, lacking in nothing."

PERSECUTION

Definition:
To cause to suffer, especially for religious or political reasons; to vex, harass on basis of race, religion, gender, sexual orientation or beliefs.

Brief Explanation:
A person who believes they are being persecuted but is in fact not can be paranoid, even paranoid schizophrenic. But a person who is truly being picked on, bullied, persecuted, harassed needs help in establishing boundaries if possible or protection if need be. Children and the elderly can both be victims of persecution, so it behooves a counselor to be on guard for such things. Just because a person says the devil is out to get them doesn't mean they are paranoid, it could be true!

The Word of God:
Matthew 5:10-12
"Blessed are those who have been persecuted for the sake of righteousness, for theirs is the kingdom of heaven. Blessed are you when people insult you and persecute you, and falsely say all kinds of evil against you because of Me. Rejoice and be glad, for your reward in heaven is great; for in the same way they persecuted the prophets who were before you."

John 15:20
"Remember the word that I said to you, 'A slave is not greater than his master.' If they persecuted Me, they will also persecute you; if they kept My word, they will keep yours also."

Romans 12:14
"Bless those who persecute you; bless and do not curse."

2 Timothy 3:12

"Indeed, all who desire to live godly in Christ Jesus will be persecuted."

PRAYER

Definition:

Prayer is the act of making a reverent petition to God, a god, or another object of worship. It is further an act of communion with God, a god, or another object of worship, such as in devotion, confession, praise, or thanksgiving. Prayer can also be seen as a religious observance in which praying predominates, and can include a fervent request.

Brief Explanation:

Prayer in counseling is expected by the Christian client, and is one of the most potent "weapons of our warfare" available to us. When I pray for a client, I try to focus on two things. First, I pray what has been discussed, with a possible solution at the end. Second, I pray with my eyes open, after the client closes their eyes, to see the response, which can be most telling.

We should pray in faith, pray with sensitivity, pray for healing and restoration, and pray the blessing of the Lord on those we minister to. Prayer, and the study of the Word are our greatest tools for ministry, and it is a privilege to pray for those we minister to. For more, see *The Prayer Training Manual* by John Delgado, and *Prayer* by Dr. Walters.

The Word of God:

Psalm 34:15,17,18

"The face of the Lord is against evildoers, To cut off the

memory of them from the earth. The righteous cry, and the Lord hears And delivers them out of all their troubles. The Lord is near to the brokenhearted And saves those who are crushed in spirit."

Matthew 6:9-13

"Pray, then, in this way: 'Our Father who is in heaven, Hallowed be Your name. Your kingdom come. Your will be done, On earth as it is in heaven. Give us this day our daily bread. And forgive us our debts, as we also have forgiven our debtors. And do not lead us into temptation, but deliver us from evil. For Yours is the kingdom and the power and the glory forever. Amen."

Matthew 21:22

"And all things you ask in prayer, believing, you will receive."

Matthew 7:7,8

"Ask, and it will be given to you; seek, and you will find; knock, and it will be opened to you. For everyone who asks receives, and he who seeks finds, and to him who knocks it will be opened."

John 15:7

"If you abide in Me, and My words abide in you, ask whatever you wish, and it will be done for you."

1 Thessalonians 5:17

"Pray without ceasing"

Philippians 4:6

"Be anxious for nothing, but in everything by prayer and supplication with thanksgiving let your requests be made known to God."

PRIDE

Definition:

Pride is a sense of one's own proper dignity or value; self-respect. It can also mean to have pleasure or satisfaction taken in an achievement, possession, or association: *parental pride.* In a negative vein, it can mean arrogant or disdainful conduct or treatment; haughtiness, often accompanied by an excessively high opinion of oneself; conceit.

Brief Explanation:

There is an old song that says "oh, Lord, it's hard to be humble, when you're perfect in everyway." Well, of course, the writer (one hopes) was writing this tongue and cheek. However, there are people who do think a bit more highly than they should of themselves and others who are not nearly as aware as they should be of the unique and special person they are. Pride is often the door through which every other area of sin enters. Having a realistic appraisal of oneself is key to a healthy self concept, which is necessary to approach life with faith and hope. Without positive pride, a person often devalues themselves to their detriment; one who overvalues oneself is setting themselves up for a fall. A counselor will graciously attempt to bring to the person in counseling a proper, balanced and honest appraisal of themselves, a first step toward mental health.

The Word of God:

Leviticus 26:19

"And I will break the pride of your strength, and will make your heavens as iron, and your earth as bronze;"

2 Chronicles 32:26

"And Hezekiah was humbled for the pride of his heart, he and the people of Jerusalem, and the wrath of Jehovah did not come on *them in the days of Hezekiah."*

Psalm 10:4

"Through pride of his face, the wicked will not seek; there is no God in all of his schemes."

Proverbs 8:13

"The fear of Jehovah is to hate evil; I hate pride and loftiness, and the evil way, and the perverse mouth."

Proverbs 11:2

"Pride comes, then shame comes, but with the lowly is wisdom."

Proverbs 13:10

"Argument only comes by pride, but wisdom is with those who take advice."

Proverbs 16:18

"Pride goes before destruction, and a haughty spirit before a fall."

1John 2:16

"Because all that which is in the world: the lust of the flesh, and the lust of the eyes, and the pride of life, is not of the Father, but is of the world."

RESURRECTION

Definition:

Resurrection is the act of rising from the dead or returning to life. It is the state of one who has returned to life. Specifically in Christianity, it is the rising again of Jesus on the third day after the Crucifixion, and the rising again of the dead at the Last Judgment.

Brief Explanation:

Belief in the resurrection is a fundamental doctrine of the church. As Christian counselors the topic of the resurrection usually only arises at the time of a death of a loved one. Being familiar with the scriptures relating to the resurrection, our blessed hope, will arm you for effective ministry.

The Word of God:

Psalm 30:3, 41:10

"O Lord, You have brought up my soul from Sheol; You have kept me alive, that I would not go down to the pit. But You, O Lord, be gracious to me and raise me up..."

John 11: 25, 26

"Jesus said to her, "I am the resurrection and the life; he who believes in Me shall live even if he dies, and everyone who lives and believes in Me shall never die. Do you believe this?"

1 Corinthians 15:3-8

"For I delivered to you as of first importance what I also received, that Christ died for our sins according to the Scriptures, and that he was buried, and that He was raised on the third day according to the Scriptures. And that He appeared to Cephas, then to the twelve. After that He appeared to more than five hundred brethren at one time, most of whom remain until now, but some have fallen asleep; then he appeared to James, then to all the apostles; and last of all, as to one untimely born, He appeared to me also."

John 14:19

"After a little while the world will no longer see Me, but you will see Me; because I live, you will live also."

REVENGE

Definition:

Revenge is defined as the inflicting of punishment in return for injury or insult. It also can mean to seek or take vengeance for oneself or another person; avenge.

Brief Explanation:

Ah, sweat revenge. Perhaps, many have such thoughts, but since the Lord certainly knew we could not be trusted with the responsibility of what is just recompense, he left revenge for his purview. Revenge is a theme you often hear in counseling and one even recommended by some in cases of child abuse. Justice is needed in many cases, but the Lord forbids us to take revenge, as it sets in motion a cycle that sadly never ceases. Helping the client to deal with the anger, hurt or pain that causes them to want to take revenge is our key to helping the client avoid the additional pain that would be caused if revenge, no matter how sweet it might feel, were acted on.

The Word of God:

Romans 12:19

"Never take you own revenge, beloved, but leave room for the wrath of God, for it is written, "Vengeance is mine, I will repay" says the Lord.

Matthew 5:38-41

"You have heard that it was said, 'An eye for an eye, and a

tooth for a tooth.' But I say to you, do not resist an evil person; but whoever slaps you on your right cheek, turn the other to him also. If anyone wants to sue you and take your shirt, let him have your coat also. Whoever forces you to go one mile, go with him two."

Matthew 6:14

"For if you forgive others for their transgressions, your heavenly Father will also forgive you."

SALVATION

Definition:

Salvation is defined as the preservation or deliverance from destruction, difficulty, or evil. It is further a source, means, or cause of such preservation or deliverance. In Christianity it is deliverance from the power or penalty of sin; redemption or the agent or means that brings about such deliverance.

Brief Explanation:

I have had, on a number of occasions, to lead someone in counseling to Christ. You must be sensitive to where a person is at, as not everyone is ready to accept Christ, though they may desperately need him, and all must be drawn by the Holy Spirit.

Yet, counselors must be prepared to share their faith with a non-believer, and also help believers who are struggling with believing that they are really are saved.

The assurance of salvation is fairly easy to ascertain. If they have confessed Christ, and believe in the resurrection, according to scripture they are saved or born again. Assisting the client to trust the veracity of scripture may be necessary, and for those who really do not know the Lord, you may be given the privilege of leading them to Christ…so be ready and prayerful. Then, be ready to refer them to a strong bible believing church, as the counseling office is rarely (since you charge for your time) the best place for discipleship, and integration into the church, baptism, etc. is essential to their continued growth. Remember, we are working in cooperation with the church, not in competition.

The Word of God:

Exodus 15:2

"The Lord is my strength and song, and He has become my salvation; This is my God, and I will praise Him; My father's God, and I will extol Him."

Isaiah 55:6

"Seek the Lord while He may be found; Call upon Him while He is near."

John 3:16-18

"For God so loved the world that He gave His only begotten Son, that everyone believing into Him should not perish, but have everlasting life. For God did not send His Son into the world that He might judge the world, but that the world might be saved through Him. The one believing into Him is not condemned; but the one not believing has already been condemned, for he has not believed into the name of the only begotten Son of God."

Romans 10:9, 10

"Because if you confess the Lord Jesus with your mouth, and believe in your heart that God raised Him from the dead, you will be saved. For with the heart one believes unto righteousness, and with the mouth one confesses unto salvation."

2 Corinthians 5:17

"Therefore if anyone is in Christ, he is a new creature; the old things passed away; behold, new things have come."

SATAN

Definition:

Satan is defined in Judeo-Christian and Islamic religions as the chief spirit of evil and adversary of God; tempter of mankind; master of Hell.

Brief Explanation: Satan and the evil he tries to spread are real and will often be encountered in the counseling office. It has been asked, I cannot remember by or to whom, if a Christian can have a demon. The answer was purported to be; "I suppose he can if he wants one". Of course, no Christian wants or would want to be demonized (the biblical word, meaning harassed, attacked, but not possessed), but many I have worked with over the years, especially severe abuse cases, have experienced great relief after prayer for deliverance.

Deliverance ministry has historically and rightly been a primary ministry of the church, and should remain as such. I am a firm believer that rarely is there a rush on seeking deliverance for a person, and that a team consisting of counselor and pastor or others trained in this specialized area of ministry works best. In either case, Satan is alive and still seeking to hurt the believer, but thank God he is a defeated foe, under our feet, and under our authority.

The Word of God:
Mark 16:17

"And miraculous signs will follow to those believing these things: they will cast out demons in My name; they will speak new languages..."

Ephesians 6:11

"Put on the full armor of God, so that you will be able to stand firm against the schemes of the devil."

James 4:7

"Submit therefore to God. Resist the devil and he will flee from you."

1 Peter 5:8, 9

"Be of sober spirit, be on the alert. Your adversary, the devil, prowls about like a roaring lion, seeking someone to devour. But resist him, firm in your faith, knowing that the same experiences of suffering are being accomplished by your brethren who are in the world."

SELF-IMAGE

Definition:

Self-image is the idea, conception, or mental image one has of oneself.

Brief Explanation:

As stated in the definition, self concept or self image is the idea, conception, or mental image one has of oneself. Every person has an image or belief about ones goodness or badness. For

example, as stated under humility, a humble person is not merely self-effacing. He or she is a person with an honest appraisal of themselves in terms of their strengths and weaknesses. They have learned to accept themselves as they are, without accepting sin or a weakness that may be overcome. As was noted above, Jesus was the meekest of all, having a quiet strength of character; he was also humble, in that he rightly knew who he was, and who he wasn't, and what he was called to do.

Self concept is developed in most people early in life, and is made up of the various experiences, good and bad that the person has had. Whether a person has a positive or negative self image is often determined by how the person evaluates their life experience...positive or negative. Further, as stated under pride, there are people who do think a bit more highly than they should of themselves and others who are not nearly as aware as they should be of the unique and special person they are.

Having a realistic appraisal of oneself is key to a healthy self concept, which is necessary to approach life with faith and hope. If a person devalues themselves, not seeing clearly that they are precious to the Lord, created in His image and likeness, or if they overvalue themselves, thinking that they are better than others, a wrong self concept and ultimate self esteem will be skewed. A counselor must help the suffering saint to see themselves in light of God's word, not based upon others appraisal or even their own.

The Word of God:

Genesis 1:26-28

"And God said, let Us make man in Our image, according to our likeness; and let them rule over the fish of the sea, and over the birds of the heavens, and over the cattle, and over all of the earth, and over all the creepers creeping on the earth. And God created the man in His own image; in the image of God He created him. He created them male and female. And God blessed them; and God said to them, be fruitful and multiply, and fill the earth, and subdue

it, and rule over the fish of the seas, and over birds of the heavens, and over all beasts creeping on the earth."

Philippians 2:5-8

"Have this attitude in yourselves which was also in Christ Jesus, who, although He existed in the form of God, did not regard equality with God a thing to be grasped, but emptied Himself, taking the form of a bond-servant, and being made in the likeness of men. Being found in appearance as a man, He humbled Himself by becoming obedient to the point of death on the cross."

2 Chronicles 7:14

"And My people who are called by My name humble themselves and pray and seek My face and turn from their wicked ways then I will hear from heaven, will forgive their sin and will heal their land."

Proverbs 15:33

"The fear of the Lord is instruction for wisdom, and before honor comes humility."

Matthew 18:4

"Whoever then humbles himself as this child, he is the greatest in the kingdom of heaven."

James 4:6

"God is opposed to the proud, but gives grace to the humble."

1 Peter 5:6

"Therefore humble yourselves under the mighty hand of God, that He may exalt you at the proper time."

Proverbs 16:18, 19

"Pride goes before destruction, And a haughty spirit before stumbling. It is better to be of a humble spirit with the lowly, Than to divide the spoil with the proud."

1 John 2:16

"For all that is in the world, the lust of the flesh and the lust of the eyes and the boastful pride of life, is not from the Father, but is from the world."

2 Samuel 18:18

"Now Absalom in his lifetime had taken and set up for himself a pillar which is in he King's Valley, for the said "I have no son to preserve my name." So he named the pillar after his own name, and is called Absalom's monument to this day."

SEXUAL IMMORALITY

Definition:

Violation of the laws of God in the sexual arena, which can include homosexuality and other sexual perversions.

Brief Explanation:

The list of areas or activities of sexual deviance or dysfunction is nearly exhaustive; it is not necessary to state them all here. However, as a counselor it is necessary to understand the various lengths some will go to satisfy their sexual urges outside of how God intended, in the bonds of marriage. God intended for man and woman to receive full and complete satisfaction and joy within the bonds of marriage. With the introduction of videos, internet, etc. access to various types of immoral content has become easier than ever, with destructive results.

As a counselor, you will often be faced with attempting to bring restoration and healing to a couple where immorality has occurred, requiring much skill to bring healing, forgiveness and the rebuilding of trust, if it is possible. Jesus acknowledged it was not always possible. Where immorality has turned to addiction, group and individual therapy, with strong accountability is often the best method of treatment. In either case, dealing with sexual sin is one of the most challenging of a counselor's role, and must be managed with care.

The Word of God:
1 Thessalonians 4:3,4,7

"For this is the will of God, your sanctification; that is, that you abstain from sexual immorality; that each of you know how to possess his own vessel in sanctification an honor, For God has not called us for the purpose of impurity, but in sanctification."

Hebrews 13:4

"Marriage is to be held in honor among all, and the marriage bed is to be undefiled; for fornicators and adulterers God will judge."

2 Peter 2:9

"...then the Lord knows how to rescue the godly from temptation, and to keep the unrighteous under punishment for the day of judgment,..."

1 Corinthians 10:13

"No temptation has overtaken you but such as is common to man; and God is faithful, who will not allow you to be tempted beyond what you are able, but with the temptation will provide the way of escape also, so that you will be able to endure it."

SHAME

Definition:

Shame is a painful emotion caused by a strong sense of guilt, embarrassment, unworthiness, or disgrace. It is often seen in one that brings dishonor, disgrace, or condemnation to themselves and/or others.

Brief Explanation:

Shame is different than guilt, which is covered in some detail previously. Shame usually is a feeling, or a conscious awareness that ones very person is not good enough, flawed, worthless. It is the experience of feeling thoroughly embarrassed at ones very core. Shame can be healthy if there is indeed something that has been done wrong by the person, and the answer for it is confession, repentance, and if necessary restitution. However, the problem often seen in counseling is in working with someone with inappropriate shame (overwhelming shame over minor things, or things they in fact did not do or were not responsible for, such as the victim of abuse) or too little shame (for a sociopath, such as a criminal or drug addict with no sense of responsibility for ones behavior). In either case, reality is what is needed, or an honest appraisal, in light of the word of God, of the behavior of the individual. It is important not to maximize or minimize shame, but lead the client to resolution of it beginning with an honest appraisal or diagnosis of the person in light of the word of God.

The Word of God:

Romans 9:33

"Just as it is written, Behold, I lay in Zion a stone of stumbling

and a rock of offense. And he who believes in Him will not be disappointed."

Isaiah 54:4,5

"Fear not, for you will not be put to shame; And do not feel humiliated, for you will not be disgraced; But you will forget the shame of your youth, And the reproach of your widowhood you will remember no more. For your husband is your Maker, Whose name is the Lord of hosts; And your Redeemer is the Holy One of Israel, Who is called the God of all the earth."

Romans 10:11

"For the Scripture says, "Whoever believes in Him will not be disappointed."

Hebrews 12:1, 2

"Therefore since we have so great a cloud of witnesses surrounding us, let us also lay aside every encumbrance, and the sin which so easily entangles us, and let us run with endurance the race that is set before us, fixing our eyes on Jesus, the author and perfecter of faith, who for the joy set before Him endured the cross, despising the shame, and has sat down at the right hand of the throne of God."

THANKFULNESS

Definition:

Thankfulness is an awareness and appreciation of a benefit received; grateful. It is often an expression of gratitude.

Brief Explanation:

Sometimes it is hard to even think of being thankful when you are depressed, lonely, hurt or afraid, as is often the condition of the counselee we are working with. Yet, thankfulness is a key to our contentment in this world, and truly, in the worst of situations, there are often things to be thankful for. Helping, with proper timing can be a blessing for the client, and a step towards the alleviation of their problems.

However we should avoid thankfulness when it is not appropriate, for instance, avoid telling a loved one who has just lost their spouse to be grateful since they are in a better place or out of pain. Life stinks sometimes, but God is good all the time; this is a healthy perspective, one which hopefully in time a client may be able to gain.

The Word of God:

1 Thessalonians 5:18

"In everything give thanks; for this is God's will for you in Christ Jesus."

Psalm 95:2

"Let us come before His presence with thanksgiving, Let us shout joyfully to Him with psalms."

Psalm 100:4

"Enter His gates with thanksgiving And His courts with praise. Give thanks to Him, bless His name."

THOUGHTS

Definition:

Thoughts is the act or process of thinking; cogitation. It is a product of thinking, which utilizes the faculty of thinking or reasoning. Further, it is intellectual activity or production of a particular time or group; such as in ancient Greek thought.

Brief Explanation:

The process of changing ones thinking or renewing the mind is a major area of counseling. Thoughts precede behavior and feelings, so the changing or regulating of thoughts is important. Thus, if the client in their mind is constantly telling themselves that they will never make it or are no good, it is no wonder that depressed mood and poor attitudes and behavior will follow.

Listening in to the thoughts of a person is an art form and much of our talk and listening to a client is designed to hear this secret dialog that goes on in the clients head. We cannot read their mind, but we can assume certain thoughts based upon the behaviors and attitudes we see. Encouraging the client to "talk out loud" their honest thoughts will help us to determine what is needed for them, what themes they are acting on, and how to intervene with words of truth and life. When we replace the negative with healthy and truthful words, spoken as seed over time, they will take root and bring forth healthy fruit in terms of thoughts that reflect Christ and produce a change in attitude and behavior. Easier said than done, but this is our quest.

The Word of God:

Proverbs 23: 7

"For as he (a person) thinks within himself, so he is."

Matthew 15:18,19

"But the things that proceed out of the mouth come from the heart, and those defile the man. For out of the heart come evil

thoughts, murders, adulteries, fornications, thefts, false witness, slanders."

Colossians 3:2

"Set your mind on the things above, not on the things that are on the earth."

Romans 12:2

"And do not be conformed to this world, but be transformed by the renewing of your mind, so that you may prove what the will of God is, that which is good and acceptable and perfect."

Philippians 2:5

"Have this attitude in yourselves which was also in Christ Jesus."

TROUBLE

Definition:

Trouble is a state of distress, affliction, difficulty, or need: also a distressing or difficult circumstance or situation. It can also be seen as effort, especially when inconvenient or bothersome, and which could cause a condition of pain, disease, or malfunction.

Brief Explanation:

"No body knows, the trouble I seen, no body knows, but Jesus." The old Negro spiritual presents a powerful truth about the lives of people coming for counseling. It is true, that everyone's troubles are uniquely theirs, but usually they are similar to others.

People often ask when trouble comes, why me? Well, why not you or me? Trouble comes...Jesus put it, in this world you will have trouble...take courage, I have overcome the world. Perhaps we could say that was easy for Jesus to say, but in fact, to overcome troubles takes courage, something often lacking in the client, and must be lent for a season by the counselor.

A counselor motivates the counselee to **face** the trouble they have head on, but not alone. We then help to **trace** the troubles to the point of origin, learn what we can about them, repent for sin and admit responsibility as needed, **erase** the trouble by our repentance (a change of thinking leading to a change in lifestyle) and hopefully **replace** the troubles with new choices that are more functional and effective.

The truth is, troubles come, and troubles go...it is better when they go.

The Word of God:

Psalm 9:9

"The Lord also will be a stronghold for the oppressed, A stronghold in times of trouble..."

Psalm 27:5

"For in the day of trouble He will conceal me in His tabernacle; In the secret place of His tent He will hide me; He will lift me up on a rock."

Psalm 31:7,9

"I will rejoice and be glad in Your lovingkindness, Because You have seen my affliction; You have known the troubles of my soul..."

Psalm 55:22

"Cast your burden upon the Lord and He will sustain you; He will never allow the righteous to be shaken."

Psalm 46:1

"God is our refuge and strength, A very present help in trouble."

Psalm 18:2,3

"The Lord is my rock and my fortress and my deliverer, My God, my rock, in whom I take refuge; My shield and the horn of my salvation, my stronghold. I call upon the Lord, who is worthy to be praised, And I am saved from my enemies."

TRUST

Definition:

Trust is a firm reliance on the integrity, ability, or character of a person or thing. It is something committed into the care of another; charge. It is also reliance on something in the future; hope.

Brief Explanation:

The first verse I learned as a child after becoming a Christian was Proverbs 3:5, 6, referenced below; trust in the Lord. I suppose this was my first because I needed to learn to trust, and had such difficulty doing so. Trust is the first stage in normal human growth, and is a necessary component of any relationship. When violated, it is the most difficult thing to regain, requiring more than forgiveness, but a rebuilding of the trust lost.

Trust is lost if we have or perceived we have been betrayed. Notice I said that the betrayal can be real or perceived, but the result will likely be the same, a breaking of trust, which makes relationship so difficult.

Since most clients will have issues surrounding trust,

establishing trust with the client is an essential component of the therapeutic relationship, and must be established early and reinforced often. We do this through our attending to the client, listening carefully, following up with promises made, etc. Thus, building trust is a key for us to be effective as counselors.

The Word of God:
Proverbs 3:5,6

"Trust in the Lord with all your heart And do not lean on your own understanding. In all your ways acknowledge Him, And He will make your paths straight."

Job 13:15

"Though He slay me, I will hope in Him. Nevertheless I will argue my ways before Him."

Romans 8:37

"But in all these things we overwhelmingly conquer through Him who loved us."

Psalm 37:3-5

"Trust in the Lord and do good; Dwell in the land and cultivate faithfulness. Delight yourself in the Lord; And he will give you the desires of your heart. Commit your way to the Lord, Trust also in Him, and he will do it."

WISDOM

Definition:

Wisdom is the ability to discern or judge what is true, right, or lasting; insight. It includes common sense; good judgment. It can be further defined as the sum of learning through the ages; knowledge, and includes wise teachings of the ancient sages.

Brief Explanation:

Knowledge gained leads to understanding, and understanding when applied leads to wisdom. The bible sees wisdom as something to be gained, to be bought, and to be held on to. It is essential akin to common sense, or knowing what to do and when to do it.

Wisdom is the practical application of biblical principles to life. Many clients will lack wisdom, which we are to ask for, in the Holy Spirit, and will be granted us if we take the time to know and understand the word of God, and are willing to walk in obedience to the word.

The Word of God:

Proverbs 1:7

"The fear of the Lord is the beginning of knowledge; Fools despise wisdom and instruction."

Psalm 1:1,2

"How blessed is the man who does not walk in the counsel of the wicked, Nor stand in the path of sinners, Nor sit in the seat of scoffers! But his delight is in the law of the Lord, And in His law he meditates day and night."

Proverbs 3:13

"How blessed is the man who finds wisdom and the man who gains understanding."

Colossians 3:16

"Let the word of Christ richly dwell within you, with all wisdom teaching and admonishing one another with psalms and hymns and spiritual songs, singing with thankfulness in your hearts to God."

WORSHIP

Definition:

Worship is the reverent love and devotion accorded a deity, an idol, or a sacred object. It includes the ceremonies, prayers, or other religious forms by which this love is expressed with ardent devotion and adoration.

Brief Explanation:

Similar to thankfulness, worship is an important component to a healthy life. Worship is accomplished through service, through the study of the word, and through singing, etc in church or at home. Worship is also an attitude of gratitude for what the Lord has done.

I have found that a true worshipper of the Lord can be down, but not for long. They can be lonely, but not for long. They can be hurt, but the healing comes as they remain in the presence of the Lord. All of our life is to be lived with a conscious presence of the Lord in our lives. I encourage every counselor to be a worshipper of the Lord, and encourage your clients to be the same. The benefits are multitudinous.

The Word of God:
Exodus 34:1"4

"...for you shall not worship any other god, for the Lord, whose name is Jealous, is a jealous God..."

Psalm 29:2

"Ascribe to the Lord the glory due to His name; Worship the Lord in holy array."

Psalm 95:6

"Come, let us worship and bow down, Let us kneel before the Lord our Maker."

Conclusion and Recommendations

There are probably many more topics that could have been provided in this book, but these were deemed by the author as the most important. The key for a counselor is to know both the principles of God's word and good common sense. Caring for another person by listening carefully and compassionately is the beginning of helping them. Using the word of God, the truth of His word, with wisdom and understanding is most powerful for the person who has an open heart to the Lord.

Referenced Books by Dr. DeKoven

Family Violence: Patterns of Destruction.

Marriage and Family Life: A Christian Perspective.

Addictions Counseling

12 Steps to Wholeness

Journey to Wholeness

Supernatural Architecture

Human Development with Dr. Joseph Bohac

Parenting on Purpose

Living Fruitfully with Dr. David Wyns

Referenced Books by Dr. Ken Chant

Building the Church God Wants

Mountain Movers

Faith Dynamics

Dazzling Secrets for Despondent Saints

To the Corinthians

Christian Life: Patterns of Gracious Living

Referenced Books by Other Authors

Off Center, Off Course by Dr. Richard Walters

Strong Prayer, Strong Man and *Strong Prayer, Strong Woman* by Dr. Richard Walters and Dr. Diane Walters respectively.

Bringing Heaven to Earth by Dr. Tim Dailey.

Resourcing the Vision: Comprehensive Guide to Stewardship by Dick Edic

The Prayer Training Manual by John Delgado

www.ingramcontent.com/pod-product-compliance
Lightning Source LLC
Chambersburg PA
CBHW050830160426
43192CB00010B/1973